SHELF
RESPECT

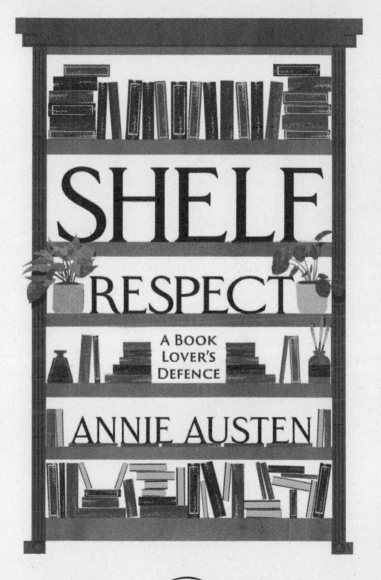

SHELF
RESPECT

A BOOK LOVER'S DEFENCE

ANNIE AUSTEN

sphere

SPHERE

First published in Great Britain in 2019 by Sphere

3 5 7 9 10 8 6 4 2

A CIP catalogue record for this book
is available from the British Library.

ISBN 978-0-7515-7867-6

Typeset in Galliard by M Rules
Printed and bound in Great Britain by
Clays Ltd, Elcograf S.p.A.

Papers used by Sphere are from well-managed forests
and other responsible sources.

Sphere
An imprint of
Little, Brown Book Group
Carmelite House
50 Victoria Embankment
London EC4Y 0DZ

An Hachette UK Company
www.hachette.co.uk

www.littlebrown.co.uk

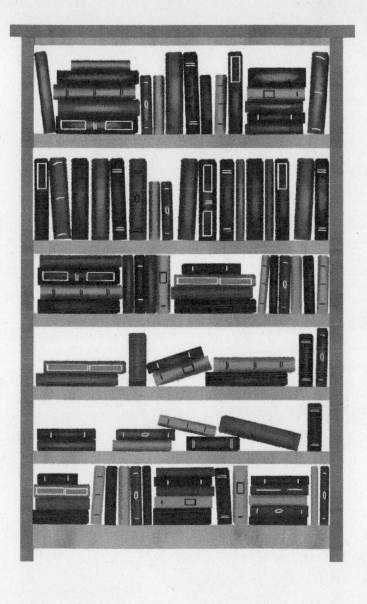

Contents

Introduction   1

What do your books say about you?   7

A dozen fictional books in literature   16

The People's Bookshelf of Latvia   20

Is it compulsory to finish a book once we've
    started it?   23

Five novels that take place over a single day   28

Ten books found on Osama Bin Laden's
    bookshelf   29

Five things Oscar Wilde said about books
    and reading   34

Dr Johnson on reading   37

Barack Obama's last presidential summer reads   41

Books selected most often by Desert Island
    Discs castaways   45

In praise of the bookcase   49

Ten genuine one-star reader reviews of classic
    literature   58

Do we really need books?   62

Five songs inspired by books   68
How to arrange your books on the shelves   69
Ten rejected titles for great books   85
A lender or borrower be?   88
Ten great quotes about books and reading   99
Strange things found in books   102
A dozen books read on screen in films   106
Death by bookcase   110
Fifteen books from the personal library of
    Marilyn Monroe   112
'The harmless and delicious fever': How
    bibliophilic are you?   115
Some notable bibliophiles   121
J.K. Rowling's favourite childhood reading   131
The merging of the book collections   132
Ten prolific authors   137
Bookshelves that made history   140
Great sliding bookcases   149
Six weird book titles   154
Bookshelves in style   155
An early dog-ear   159
The horse librarians of Kentucky   161
Five fictional bookshops   165
Five great cinema bookshelves   166
A great fictional library   173
The Brownings' bookcase   176
Ten fictional places in literature   178
All Greek to us   181

Introduction

In the autumn of 2017 *Ideal Home* magazine ran a home-decor feature about a real dwelling occupied by real, sentient humans that included a photograph of a set of bookshelves where the books had all been placed with the pages facing outwards. The spines of the books were against the wall, meaning people in the room were left looking at a featureless line of beige page-ends. What kind of madness was this? In other photographs the art hadn't been turned to face the wall and all the furniture seemed to be facing the right way, so was this a simple yet terrible mistake in set-dressing like a rogue cardboard coffee cup among the flagons in *Game of Thrones*?

Apparently not. These books had been deliberately placed with the pages facing outwards, rendering them anonymous and making the shelves look, well, *weird*.

It was like a void had appeared where books should be, an idiosyncratic blandness that served only to draw attention to a curious vacancy in the room. It was as if the books on the shelf had been reduced to an eerie, almost shameful silence. Nothing in the pages of *Ideal Home* has ever looked more wrong than the backwards books. It was an affront, a provocation, a scandal. There's even a fair-to-middling chance that displaying books with the pages facing outwards contravenes the Geneva Convention on the grounds of sensory deprivation.

For anyone who loves books, this was as bewildering as it was utterly dismaying. Why would anyone think such a heinous act of self-imposed domestic cultural censorship was in any way a good idea? It's bonkers on the most practical level – what happens if you're sitting there one day and think, 'I'm in the mood for a bit of Maupassant, or maybe some E.L. James'? How on earth are you going to find it? Unless you happen upon it first time with a lucky guess, the inevitable consequence is you ending up on your knees and sobbing, surrounded by a jumble of books.

Even putting aside such practicalities, what person in their right mind would want to hide their books

like this, especially to produce arguably the blandest, most soul-sapping colour of them all – beige? It's like a football fan going to the match and spending the entire ninety minutes facing the back wall of the stand, or someone going to see their favourite band and spending the entire gig with their eyes closed and their fingers in their ears. Would you store your CDs and DVDs *sans* covers and filed with the blank sides of the discs facing forward? No. No, you would not; if you did, your friends would consider staging some kind of intervention.

The idea of storing one's books with their pages outwards is the stuff of nightmares, enough to have any bibliophile worth their salt waking up in the middle of the night distressed and shouting. You'd almost prefer someone to give their books away rather than conceal their identities like this. We are a proud literary people and this is a warning shot across the bows from the philistines. Before we know it their tanks won't just be on our lawns, they'll be in our libraries.

If our books retain one thing – even if they're dog-eared and their pages are swollen by an unfortunate bathing incident, even if we don't pick them up or open them for years – it's their dignity. Show their underbellies in this way and that dignity is removed entirely by an act as simple as a turn of 180 degrees. There's an inherent cruelty in displaying books at their most vulnerable like this, their bloomers showing, their skirts tucked into their drawers, an affront to something that's taken months, if not years, to produce and make as perfect as can be.

To so blatantly disrespect books like this is essentially a form of bullying. They're bullying our books, my friends, and we need to resist the bullies. Let us stand with our books, be proud of our reading and show solidarity with our Ikea Billys. It's time to celebrate the bookshelf and honour the bookcase. Let's wave the flag for our bibliophilia and be unashamed about our domestic libraries. The time has come – indeed it is long overdue – to restore to our literary legacies a bit of shelf-respect.

'Ah, how good it is to be among people who are reading.'

Rainer Maria Rilke

What do your books say about you?

Alan Bennett summed up succinctly the meaning of books displayed on shelves while considering how books and bookcases are used as set-dressing in his plays and films. (Set designers often present him with units stuffed with the kind of old gilt-lettered volumes found today only in gentlemen's clubs and stately homes or randomly selected junk volumes from remainder shops.) A case of books is as revealing about its owner as their clothes, he said, and a personality is shaped around a library 'just as a shoe is shaped to the foot'.

Most of us, when visiting someone's home for the first time, will be drawn to their bookshelves. For people like us, first literary impressions count as much as general first impressions, if not more. Casting an eye over someone's bookshelf is the last acceptable form of social intrusion, falling safely between a basic enquiry after someone's health and scrolling through their text messages when they've popped to the loo.

Bookshelves are a shortcut to a person, as if their psyche is showing its workings. How relieved we are when we find volumes that we own ourselves, especially if they're among our favourites. How interested we are to see writers we've never heard of, or a complete set of books by a particular author we've been meaning to explore ourselves. Conversely, how our heart sinks when we see a selection of books in a genre we don't enjoy, or even one we actively dislike. It's a feeling similar to that when someone you like is rude to waiting staff. 'Noooo,' we want to cry, 'I thought we were going to be friends!'

Worst of all, how dismaying is it when we find no books at all? We're not the kind of people who are quick to judge* but a total absence of books should ring alarm bells and possibly require some kind of prearranged safe word to be whispered into a microphone

---

* Yes, we are.

8

concealed behind a lapel. There's nothing inherently wrong with a house being completely devoid of books* but it does raise certain questions about the kind of person we're dealing with. It's surely a near-impossible task to keep a house devoid of any books whatsoever; someone would have to work pretty hard to banish them entirely from their home. It would take some kind of grudge against books to completely book-proof a residence – after all, they just seem to gravitate there almost by osmosis. How many of us have found books on our shelves we've no recollection of acquiring, for example? They just arrive. They turn up. And then they multiply. Maintaining a book-free home would take considerable effort: spreading some kind of powder under the window frames, say, or keeping a repellent spray under the sink.

People's book collections are intimate things and in being granted access to them, even tangentially by the act of being invited into someone's home, you're being allowed in to the history of someone's introspection, the time they've spent alone with themselves being entertained, educated, comforted, provoked, improved

---

* Yes, there is.

and consoled. When a person reads, they are unadulterated and undiluted, entirely without pretence. Someone's bookshelves are a way of showing you who they are, a presentation of themselves that is at once personal and shared. There's a mutual trust involved in the scanning of a bookshelf that's crucial to any successful relationship from superficial friendship to lifelong romance.

Which all goes to show why people with no books in their house are not to be trusted. As John Waters wisely advised, 'If you go home with somebody and they don't have books, don't fuck 'em.' What are they hiding? Get out of there, fast.

But what of ourselves? What do our shelves say about us? Can we detect a tangible, even helpful self-awareness in our acquisitions and the manner in which we store and display them? On the face of it, our bookshelves and bookcases contain rows of rationally chosen titles that we've read critically – sometimes dispassionately, sometimes completely absorbed – and placed back among the rest of our books. Superficially there's an equality there, a democracy of selection and circumstances. Go a little deeper, though, and there's much more than that.

ULYSSES

JAMES JOYCE

A BRIEF HISTORY OF TIME

STEVEN HAWKING

TOLSTOY

WAR & PEACE

DAVID FOSTER WALLACE

INFINITE JEST

A TALE OF TWO CITIES

CHARLES DICKENS

HAMLET

SHAKESPEARE

OF MICE AND MEN

JOHN STEINBECK

THE COLLECTED POEMS OF WILLIAM WORDSWORTH

FAR FROM THE MADDING CROWD

HARDY

THE CANTERBURY TALES

GEOFFREY CHAUCER

HARPER LEE

TO KILL A MOCKINGBIRD

SAPIENS

HARARI

NORMAL PEOPLE

SALLY ROONEY

ELEANOR OLIPHANT IS COMPLETELY FINE

HONEYMAN

DAN BROWN

THE DA VINCI CODE

HARRY POTTER

J.K. ROWLING

Fifty Shades of Grey

E.L. James

Stand in front of your bookshelves, tilt your head to the right and run your forefinger along their contents. What do you see? Just your books? Or something more? Look a bit closer: there are the favourite books you've read so many times that the title and author on the spine are almost illegible for creases and scuffs. There are the books you bought ages ago and are still meaning to get around to. There are the books relatives have given you over several Christmases that you'll never read but can't throw away because that great-aunt or brother-in-law will notice their gift has disappeared. There are the books you had as a child that you read so often you can still almost recite them cover to cover without having to open their pages. There are the books you haven't read yet but bought simply because you were the only person in the shop and were too embarrassed to leave without buying anything after browsing for half an hour. There are the books you bought at a favourite author's book launch or festival event that you queued nervously with for ages as they sat at the table patiently inscribing and when it came to your turn you tried to think of something witty to say but panicked and blurted out, 'Just sign it to Karen, please.' (You don't know anyone called Karen.) There are the books that you bought because they were a favourite of someone you once loved. There are the books you bought because everyone else was buying and raving about them (but you didn't think were all that, to be honest). There are the books you bought because you thought they'd look cool on the shelf. There are the books you bought at the airport that ended up saving an otherwise disastrous holiday. There are the books that belonged to a grandparent that still have their name written on the flyleaf with a date long before you were born. There are the books you borrowed ages ago but can't remember who from, causing you unfeasible levels of guilt about not returning them. There are the books you found left on a train. There are the books you had to study at school and hated but that you loved when you read them as a grown-up. There are the books you don't remember buying. There are the books written by someone you know, of whom you were massively proud. There are the books you started but didn't finish. There are the books you had to get for that book club you went to for a while. There are the books you've kept for your children even if you don't have any yet. There are the books you picked up in that amazing second-hand bookshop you stumbled across in that village – what was the name of it again? There are the books you were so excited about that you pre-ordered them weeks before they were published. There are the books that guided you around that continent. There are the books that remind you of that person. There are the books that remind you of that summer. There are the books that got you through that terrible time.

Your bookshelves are not just a place where you keep your books. They are a physical manifestation of the inner you. Your library is also your autobiography.

'Literature is my Utopia. Here I am not disenfranchised. No barrier of the senses shuts me out from the sweet, gracious discourses of my book friends. They talk to me without embarrassment or awkwardness.'

Helen Keller

A dozen fictional books in literature

Darts: Master the Discipline
(*London Fields* by Martin Amis)

How to Survive 101 Calamities
(*The Poisonwood Bible* by Barbara Kingsolver)

Fifty-three More Things to do in Zero Gravity
(*The Hitchhiker's Guide to the Galaxy* by
Douglas Adams)

Pard-spirit: A Study of Branwell Brontë
(*Cold Comfort Farm* by Stella Gibbons)

A dozen fictional books in literature

Big Julie Criscoll Versus the Whole Wide World
(*One Day* by David Nicholls)

The Clue of the Broken Match
(*The Body in the Library* by Agatha Christie)

*Grammatical Garden or the Arbour of
Accidence pleasantlie open'd to Tender Wits*
(*Prince Caspian* by C.S. Lewis)

*Dropping in on Jerry: A Light-Hearted Account
of the Dresden Bombings*
(*What a Carve Up!* by Jonathan Coe)

*Life, Letters, and Labours of Miss Jane Ann
Stamper, forty-fourth edition*
(*The Moonstone* by Wilkie Collins)

The Ghastly Ordeal of Timothy Cavendish
(*Cloud Atlas* by David Mitchell)

Shelf Respect

The Dynamics of an Asteroid by Professor James Moriarty
    (*The Valley of Fear* by Arthur Conan Doyle)

Hypnotism As A Device To Uncover The Unconscious Drives And Mechanism In An Effort To Analyse the Functions Involved Which Gives Rise To Emotional Conflicts In the Waking State
       ('Sleepy Time' by P.G. Wodehouse)

'When I am attacked by gloomy thoughts, nothing helps me so much as running to my books. They quickly absorb me and banish the clouds from my mind.'

Montaigne

The People's
Bookshelf of Latvia

The atrium of Latvia's National Library in Riga on the west bank of the Daugava river is dominated by the 'People's Bookshelf', a towering bookcase rising to a height of five storeys containing volumes donated by the Latvian people. It was completed in time for the celebration of Latvia's centenary in 2018, and every member of the government presented a book that meant something to them personally. Visiting heads of state and foreign dignitaries are asked to donate a book to the People's Bookshelf: Prince Edward presented a history of Windsor Castle and Pope Francis a four-volume set of the Gospels. The library itself – completed in 2017 at a cost of $195million and resembling a sort of squashed Matterhorn with windows and a crown on top – was designed by architect Gunnar Birkerts to reflect the old Latvian folk tale 'The Princess on the Glass Mountain', a story adopted by Latvians at the start of the twentieth century as representative of their national awakening.

'A good book is the precious life-blood of a master spirit, embalmed and treasured up on purpose to a life beyond life.'

John Milton

Is it compulsory to finish a book once we've started it?

Some people are hard taskmasters, insisting on finishing a book they've started even when it's not one they're particularly enjoying. It's become clear within a handful of pages that the book is not really their thing but they've resolved to batter on through until they reach the end, at which point they'll set it aside and be immediately awash with regret at so much time ill-spent.

Time-poor as we are these days, it seems a curious act of self-flagellation to force ourselves to finish a book just because we've started it. Would we do the same with a foodstuff we don't like? Keep munching through a quantity of sprouts day after day on the

grounds that we ate one and therefore have to eat the lot, no matter how long it takes? We set out to walk to the shops and fifty yards up the road the heavens open. Do we press on, insisting that we have to now go to the shops and back in a monsoon simply because we've stepped out of the front door? Or do we just hotfoot it home again, muttering some imaginative swearwords as we go?

No, life is too short to read books we don't enjoy. There are books we just don't finish, not necessarily because we're not enjoying them. Most of us will have at least one book on the shelf with a receipt, train ticket or even a proper bookmark about a quarter of the way in where circumstances prevented us from finishing it at that particular time. Perhaps work commitments intervened, or the end of a journey, and by the time we're able to go back to a bit of reading someone's lent us a fabulous-looking new book they've raved about and we feel obliged to read it and give it back as soon as we can.

Books are not things that have to have a strict one-by-one chronological usage progression any more than clothes are. You wouldn't wear the same pair of trousers every day until they wore out (you'd be whiffy within days, for a start, and social invitations would soon dry up), so why feel you have to submit yourself to the tyranny of a bad book? That sounds like a wholly unnecessary form of self-inflicted purgatory. As Dr Johnson replied when told that a book once started should be read all the way through, 'This is surely a strange advice; you may as well resolve that whatever men you happen to get acquainted with you are to keep them for life. A book may be good for nothing; or there may be only one thing in it worth knowing; are we to read it all through?'

There is no shame in not finishing a book. If you do feel shamed by it don't just hammer away at the pages, read something else and justify it by telling yourself you haven't finished it *yet*. You'll get around to it again one day. Probably.

'Read not to contradict and confute; nor to believe and take for granted; nor to find talk and discourse; but to weigh and consider. Some books are to be tasted, others to be swallowed, and some few to be chewed and digested: that is, some books are to be read only in parts, others to be read, but not curiously, and some few to be read wholly, and with diligence and attention.'

Francis Bacon

Five novels that take place over a single day

Saturday by Ian McEwan

After Dark by Haruki Murakami

Ulysses by James Joyce

One Day in the Life of Ivan Denisovich by Aleksandr Solzhenitsyn

Mrs Dalloway by Virginia Woolf

Ten books found on
Osama Bin Laden's bookshelf

It's a little alarming to know that as bibliophiles we share a passion with some of history's most despicable characters. Hitler, who seemed outwardly to derive more pleasure from burning books than reading them, had a personal library running to more than 16,000 volumes from highfalutin monographs on art and architecture to a complete set of novels by Karl May, a German writer who turned out dodgy cowboy stories of the American West. Stalin's personal library stood at 11,000 volumes at the time of his death and he ordered books from the Kremlin's library at a rate of more than 500 a year. (How many of them subsequently ended up in his personal library is open to speculation – calling in overdue books and issuing fines to Comrade Stalin sounds a sure-fire way of earning a one-way ticket to the salt mines.) On Robert Mugabe's shelves could be found *Brideshead Revisited*, *The Idiot's Guide to Learning Latin* and Tony Blair's autobiography *A Journey*. Ever wondered about Colonel Gaddafi's favourite book, incidentally? It was *The Bridges of Madison County* by Robert James Waller.

In 2011 when US Navy Seals stormed Osama Bin Laden's compound in Abbottabad, Pakistan, the clear-up operation allowed unprecedented insights into the al-Qaeda leader, not least by the contents of his book-shelves. As well as the predictable religious tracts, a number of English-language books were discovered, revealing that Bin Laden wasn't exactly a light reader. There were no guilty pleasures at all – no TV tie-ins, no airport blockbusters, indeed no fiction at all, not even a solitary Dan Brown. If his books are anything to go by, Osama Bin Laden was not, it's safe to say, much craic. Possibly the only book he owned that might have reduced him to a fit of helpless giggles was *America's Strategic Blunders* by Willard Matthias. Other than that page-turning rib-tickler it was all pretty heavy stuff. Among his literary collection could be found:

Ten books found on Osama Bin Laden's bookshelf

Handbook of International Law by Anthony Aust

Bloodlines of the Illuminati by Fritz Springmeier

The Secrets of the Federal Reserve by Eustace Mullins

Obama's Wars by Bob Woodward

Christianity and Islam in Spain 756-1031 by C.R. Haines

The Rise and Fall of the Great Powers by Paul Kennedy

Confessions of an Economic Hit Man by John Perkins

A Brief Guide to Understanding Islam by I.A. Ibrahim

In Pursuit of Allah's Pleasure by Dr Naahah Ibrahim, Asim Abdul Maajid and Esaam-ud-Deen Darbaalah

The Secret Teachings of All Ages by Manly Hall

A lot of heavy reading there, enough to leave a chap feeling a bit drained, in fact, so it's no wonder that also found in the Bin Laden library was John Berardi's and Michael Fry's *The Grappler's Guide to Sports Nutrition.*

'Books serve to show a man that those original thoughts of his aren't very new after all.'

Abraham Lincoln

Five things Oscar Wilde said about books and reading

'It is what you read when you don't have to that determines what you will be when you can't help it.'

'There is no such thing as a moral or an immoral book. Books are well written, or badly written. That is all.'

'If one cannot enjoy reading a book over and over again, there is no use in reading it at all.'

Five things Oscar Wilde said about books and reading

'A writer is someone who has taught his mind
to misbehave.'

'I never travel without my diary. One should
always have something sensational to read on
the train.'

'The only end of writing is to
enable the readers better to enjoy life,
or better to endure it.'

Samuel Johnson

Dr Johnson on reading

'It is difficult to enumerate the several motives which procure to books the honour of perusal: spite, vanity, and curiosity, hope and fear, love and hatred, every passion which incites to any other action, serves at one time or other to stimulate a reader.

'Some are fond to take a celebrated volume into their hands, because they hope to distinguish their penetration, by finding faults which have escaped the publick; others eagerly buy it in the first bloom of reputation, that they may join the chorus of praise, and not lag, as Falstaff terms it, in "the reward of the fashion".

'Some read for style, and some for argument: one has little care about the sentiment, he observes only how it is expressed; another regards not the conclusion, but is diligent to mark how it is inferred; they read for other purposes than the attainment of practical knowledge; and are no more likely to grow wise by an examination of a treatise of moral prudence, than an architect to inflame his devotion by considering attentively the proportions of a temple.

'Some read that they may embellish their conversation, or shine in dispute; some that they may not be detected in ignorance, or want the reputation of literary accomplishments: but the most general and prevalent reason of study is the impossibility of finding another amusement equally cheap or constant, equally independent on the hour or the weather. He that wants money to follow the chase of pleasure through her yearly circuit, and is left at home when the gay world rolls to Bath or Tunbridge; he whose gout compels him to hear from his chamber the rattle of chariots transporting happier beings to plays and assemblies, will be forced to seek in books a refuge from himself.

'The author is not wholly useless, who provides innocent amusements for minds like these. There are, in the present state of things, so many more instigations to evil, than incitements to good, that he who keeps men in a neutral state, may be justly considered as a benefactor to life.'

—Samuel Johnson in *The Adventurer*,
26 February 1754

===

'The love of books is among the choicest gifts of the gods.'

Arthur Conan Doyle

===

Barack Obama's last presidential summer reads

There has probably never been a more bibliophilic US president than Barack Obama. Thomas Jefferson might run him close at least in terms of quantity – when the Library of Congress was burned down by British soldiers in 1812 Jefferson donated his personal library to replace it – but Obama was that rare thing: a political leader with his finger on the literary pulse. As such, the annual announcement of the books he had lined up for his summer reading was always eagerly anticipated. Here are the books he chose for his valedictory selection in 2016.

Shelf Respect

Barbarian Days: A Surfing Life by William Finnegan

The Girl on the Train by Paula Hawkins

H is for Hawk by Helen Macdonald

Seveneves by Neal Stephenson

The Underground Railroad by Colson Whitehead

'A good book is an event in my life.'

Stendhal

Books selected most often by Desert Island Discs castaways

Every castaway on the long-running BBC radio programme is, whether they like it or not, given a bible and a *Complete Works of Shakespeare* to take with them. They are also allowed one title of their own choice that, as the ultimate distillation of a personal library, should tell us as much about their character and personality as the eight records in their washed-up seaman's trunk. Only two guests have ever declined to choose a book: showjumper Harvey Smith in 1971 on the grounds he'd never read one, and Jamie Oliver when he appeared on the programme in 2001. 'I don't actually read books, which makes me sound pig ignorant,' said Oliver, who is dyslexic. 'I fall asleep.'

Some guests choose their solitary volume pragmatically. Barry Manilow chose *Born Survivor* by Bear Grylls, and Sandi Toksvig selected *The Ashley Book of Knots* for their practical applications, while Debbie Harry picked *War and Peace* because its length meant it would take up a lot of time. John Peel decided on a twelve-volume set of Anthony Powell's *A Dance to the Music of Time* for a similar reason: once he'd finished all twelve he would have forgotten the beginning and could start again afresh. Engelbert Humperdinck, meanwhile, plumped for his own autobiography.

The ten most frequently selected books since castaways were first asked to choose one in 1951 are:

The Divine Comedy by Dante Alighieri

Pride and Prejudice by Jane Austen

A History of the English-Speaking Peoples by Winston Churchill

Robinson Crusoe by Daniel Defoe

Books selected most often by Desert Island Discs castaways

The History of the Decline and Fall of the Roman Empire by Edward Gibbon

The Wind in the Willows by Kenneth Grahame

The Iliad/The Odyssey by Homer

À la recherche du temps perdu by Marcel Proust

Lord of the Rings by J.R.R. Tolkien

War and Peace by Leo Tolstoy

'Reading is my favourite occupation, when
I have leisure for it and books to read.'

Anne Brontë

In praise of the bookcase

In 2018 home-decor retailer Habitat announced that its sales of bookshelves and bookcases were up by 43 per cent on the previous year, which was good news for Habitat, booksellers, bibliophiles and joiners alike. Indeed, furniture retailers across the land confirmed similar rises in bookcase sales and, while it was too much of a leap to say that reading had suddenly become nearly half as popular again in the space of twelve months, this was still pretty sensational stuff. It doesn't seem to be a mere blip either: in 2017 John Lewis reported a 10 per cent increase in the sales of its bookcases and bookshelves, with its bestselling unit – a mango wood and black steel construction retailing at a whisper under £700 – rising by 244 per cent in a single year.

'Customers are falling back in love with the romanticism of collecting books and are buying beautiful shelves and display units to keep them on,' the company said over the sound of ringing tills.

Sales at high-end high-street shops like Habitat and John Lewis may have dramatically increased but there's no question as to who is the big player on the scene. Eclipsing other famous Billys – Joel, Connolly, Bob Thornton, Idol, the Kid – is the mainstay of many a modern home: the Billy bookcase produced by Ikea.

Affordable, sturdy, simply designed and – in theory, at least – easy to assemble, more than 110 million Billy bookcases have been sold worldwide since the first one rolled off its Swedish production line in 1979. Currently the Billy bookcase sells somewhere north of seven million a year, which is a lot of bookcases (not to mention an unthinkable number of those tiny pins that you hammer in to keep the back panels on). In Britain alone nearly 600,000 units are sold every year, theoretically providing shelf space for something like 90 million books. Every year. Every *year*.

The man behind the bookcase, as it were, was Gillis Lundgren, the fourth employee in the history of Ikea when he joined in 1953 and a man whose work was deemed so notable that, on his death in 2016 at the age of eighty-six, obituaries ran in newspapers all round the world. He designed the Billy bookcase, he said, on the back of a napkin. It wasn't his only design for the company – indeed, many credit him with inventing the entire concept of flat-pack furniture when he told Ikea founder Ingvar Kamprad that a table they were trying to fit into the boot of a car would be much easier to deal with if they unscrewed the legs – but it's by far the most popular and enduring of his designs. So popular and enduring indeed that financial data analysts Bloomberg devised the Bloomberg Billy Bookcase Index, comparing its prices in thirty-eight different countries to illustrate in real terms fluctuations in exchange rates.

It's not too much of a leap to say that the Billy bookcase has if not prompted then at least facilitated the popularity of books, especially in recent years when digital reading briefly looked set to take over from the printed book. With a price in double figures even for the standard large model, the Billy scores over those units sold by the likes of Habitat whose tall oak bookcases are of excellent quality but cost several hundred pounds. By being far more affordable and reasonably straightforward to build – so that even the most ham-fisted DIY-er can construct a sturdy, simple and reliable bookcase – the Billy has transformed domestic library space.

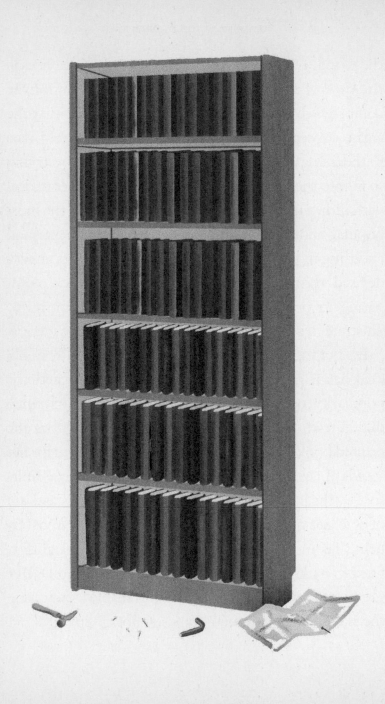

Bookcases and shelving are crucial to the dissemination of literature: in the 1930s when the US was building simple and affordable housing for working-class people, publishers actively lobbied for them to include bookshelves as a standard fitting on the grounds that empty shelves were far more likely to have people buying books to fill them rather than no shelves at all – the archetypal 'if you build it, they will come'. The importance of bookshelves to British social improvement can be gauged from the fact that in the years following the Second World War every film made by the influential Children's Film Foundation had to include bookshelves in scenes set in children's bedrooms and domestic living rooms.

Books not only furnish a room, they furnish a mind, with bookshelves our mental showrooms. In recent years bookshelves have become literal showrooms thanks to the rise of the shelfie. A term first coined in 2013, the shelfie – a photograph of your bookshelves, posted on social media – is either a mutual sharing online of your beloved books with likeminded others or one of the most egregious examples of twenty-first-century internet narcissism, depending on your point of view. The rise in sales of bookcases prompts a chicken-and-egg discussion as to whether the shelfie triggered the rising popularity of bookcases or simply reflects it, but the origin doesn't necessarily matter. The most important thing here is the increased opportunity to have a nose at people's bookshelves without leaving our own sofas.

The shelfie truly ballooned during 2018, with another flurry appearing at the start of 2019 after the tidying guru Marie Kondo suggested during her Netflix series *Tidying Up With . . .* that people discard any books they find on their shelves that don't bring them joy. Unusually for social media, the reaction was a typhoon of searingly hot takes based on a barely digested understanding of Kondo's methodology, which descended into a shriek-fest of tantrums and flouncing indignation. This response implied Kondo had demanded all books be removed from every home, placed into a flotilla of barges, towed out to the middle of the Atlantic and petrol-bombed from a fleet of helicopters. In actual fact, all Kondo had done was ask a couple who had called her in for advice on decluttering to look at their bookshelves and ask themselves, 'By having these books, will it be beneficial to my life going forward?'

Now, of course the obvious answer to this is 'duh,

#Shelfie #bookstagram #booklover #shelfrespect

yeah', but not everyone is a passionate bibliophile and, more pertinently, not everyone has the space to accommodate reams and reams of books. Let's face it, social media wouldn't be social media without massive, ill-informed, hysterical pile-ons, and the positive side to the kerfuffle was the upswing in photographs being posted of people's bookshelves. The number of Instagram posts tagged with the #shelfie hashtag at the time of writing is somewhere north of 1.6million. That's a lot of shelves and even more books.

She might not have intended it, but Marie Kondo facilitated a welcome and overdue focus on the bookshelf itself, the pictures ranging from carefully curated, lit and filtered portraits featuring books designed to show their owners in the hippest and coolest way possible, to scruffy piles of books and magazines behind ashtrays and empty lager tins. It was a tremendous celebration of the personal library, not least for its opportunity to judge the reading habits and furniture tastes of complete strangers, and one that also prompts questions about the manner in which people store, display and categorise their collections of books.

'No furniture is so charming as books.'

Sydney Smith

Ten genuine one-star reader reviews of classic literature

'First of all, the whole thing is almost all dialogue.'
> *Romeo and Juliet* by William Shakespeare

––––––

'Reminded me of Hemingway's *The Great Gatsby* which I also didn't like.'
> *Breakfast at Tiffany's* by Truman Capote

'Ever since women (deservedly) got the vote, feminists have had to scrounge for stuff to gripe about. Take Ally McBeal, for example.'
> *The Handmaid's Tale* by Margaret Atwood

Ten genuine one-star reader reviews of classic literature

'This is a tough book to read unless you understand several languages and are on LSD.'

Ulysses by James Joyce

'You know how your [sic] supposed to feel all deep and intelligent after you read a classic book. Nope, didn't happen.'

Beloved by Toni Morrison

'Everyone cheats on everyone and in the end nobody ends up happy and the audience doesn't even end up with a moral to hold on to and justify the waste of time and money they just spent.'

The Great Gatsby by F. Scott Fitzgerald

'Twee, grisly and fawning, the greatest turkey ever told.'

A Christmas Carol by Charles Dickens

'He killed innocent people, cheated on his wife and ate his friends. I believe that says it all about who Odysseus really is.'

The Odyssey by Homer

'Reading became boring, too descriptive about gardens, the streets, the town and too many characters. Not enough courtroom follow-up that could have occurred in the form of an appeal even if Mr Robinson was dead.'

To Kill a Mockingbird by Harper Lee

'Not gods, not men, nor even booksellers
have put up with poets being second rate.'

Horace

Do we really need books?

For all that we love them, books are hugely impractical when they start being gathered together in significant numbers. We probably spend somewhere between two and a dozen hours of our lives with each one, and most of them we probably only make use of once. Even our solid-gold favourites that we read again and again are in our hands for just a few hours spread over a lifetime. We read them, we stick them back on the shelf and that's where they stay, spine outwards, among the ranks of other volumes we've accumulated over the years, just taking up room. Is there an argument in favour of giving up the ones we've read and know we'll probably never read again? Imagine the space we'd save. We don't keep our daily newspapers, we don't keep most of our magazines, so what's the big deal about keeping books?

OK, that's dangerous talk, I know. Even considering the idea is enough to make the world shift a little on its axis for your average bibliophile, fearing that just the thought of it might be enough to have their library folding up into itself and disappearing like the house at the end of *Poltergeist*, but it's a pertinent question all the same. Why do we keep books when we don't keep similar items of bound paper covered in words? Well, for a start, there's more of an investment in books. Not so much in the sense of handing over cash for them, but that when we acquire a book – whether it's from a huge multinational online retailer, the chain store in the high street or a little second-hand place off the beaten track – we're saying to ourselves, 'I am going to invest in this volume something that's hard to put an actual price on: my time. This is an item that will take up physical space in my world as well as my mind and imagination.' A newspaper or magazine is largely there to provide an intake of information. Some of it might provoke further thought, disagreement and analysis, but sitting down with a book is something notably different.

Other forms of printed matter are there to fill time; a book is there to help you create it.

Also there is little chance of attaching any kind of sentimentality or deeper meaning to the act of owning a copy of *Take a Break* or the *New Statesman*. Many people do keep and file their magazines, some are even lovingly kept in binders, and interestingly many of those purpose-built binders are designed to look like books. Books denote longevity of possession, even permanence. Their publication date is hidden away on an inside page among lots of small print about moral rights, fonts and copyrights; periodicals flaunt their topicality and, by extension, ephemerality on their front covers.

Hence selling, giving away or even throwing away a book are all acts that require great consideration and are not done lightly. This month's *Vanity Fair*, though? Well, you've read the bits you want to read, so just drop it in the recycling.

Most of us will have at least attempted to pare down our collection at some point, whether because of a house move or because we've just discovered we can cross entire rooms walking on books without actually touching the floor and have forgotten what colour the carpet is. Paring down our collection is a tough task, though – one that requires the kind of immense self-discipline that the sheer amount of books we have suggests we don't possess. Isabel Allende has floor-to-ceiling shelves filled with leather-bound classics her husband has collected for years, but once a year she has a clear-out and gives loads of books away. Sheryl Sandberg keeps everything, and even still has her college textbooks 'just in case I have a sudden urge to read Schopenhauer's *The World as Will and Representation.*'

This kind of thing means that book lovers trying Marie Kondo's method of assessing each book and asking if it's adding joy to their life will most likely produce answers ranging from 'yes' through 'proba-bly' to 'ah here, give us a chance, I haven't read that one yet.' Yet even if you can't find a solitary book to take to the charity shop next time you're in town, you're still doing exactly what Marie Kondo suggests: keeping the books that bring you joy. Not in the sense of whooping and fist-pumping at the sight of each spine as you pass along the shelves, but in the stories their pages contain and the stories of how you came to own each book in the first place. The joy we find in our personal libraries, and hence the reason they are so hideously difficult to pare down, derives from the memories of what's between the covers and the circumstances by which we came to own and open those covers.

*A good book is the purest essence
of the human soul.'*

Thomas Carlyle

Five songs inspired
by books

'Wuthering Heights' by Kate Bush
Wuthering Heights by Emily Brontë

'Are Friends Electric?' by Gary Numan
Do Androids Dream of Electric Sheep? by
Philip K. Dick

'Sympathy for the Devil' by The Rolling Stones
The Master and Margarita by Mikhail Bulgakov

'Red Right Hand' by Nick Cave and the Bad Seeds
Paradise Lost by John Milton

'Killing an Arab' by The Cure
The Outsider by Albert Camus

How to arrange your
books on the shelves

The real challenge for book lovers is not in whether to dispose of books but in how to display them most effectively.

It's always a pretty laid-back affair when bibliophiles get together. Nobody gets pinned to the wall by the throat during a heated discussion about Jane Austen's best novel, and it's probably not just down to sheer chance that we've never had to solemnly commemorate The Great Font Wars. Fisticuffs rarely ensue when people chat about their favourite endpaper designs, and book clubs generally don't see their members frisked for weapons on the way in.

The only time bibliophiles become exercised – sometimes to the extent of lips being pursed and even the perceptible raising of a querulous eyebrow – is when it comes to methods of categorising books on shelves. There is no accepted 'right' way and no definite 'wrong' ways (beyond arranging them with the pages facing outwards, of course, which is for maniacs), but there are several different methods with their own advantages and disadvantages. Let's examine some of them.

Alphabetical by title

This would seem, on the face of it, to be the most obvious method of categorising books. When you want to find a specific title you can home in on it straight away with no lip-chewing, frowning or saying, 'I thought I saw it here the other day. Yes, I'm *sure* I saw it here the other day.' It's also a system that's sympathetic to browsing and encouraging serendipity: a volume of poetry you've not looked at in ages will catch your eye between that challenging slab of literary fiction and the pacy, readable history of the American Civil War you'd actually gone looking for. The disadvantages of storing books alphabetically by title is that if you have more than one book by the same author then their work is scattered far and wide like orphaned children.

Armistead Maupin's *Tales of the City*, for example, would not only be separated from its immediate sequel *More Tales of the City*, but it would also come after it on the shelves when it should come before. The entire nine-volume set would be all over the place, higgledy and indeed piggledy. It's practically anarchy. The spines of Peter Guralnick's two-volume biography of Elvis Presley, *Last Train to Memphis* and *Careless Love*, when placed together form a portrait of the singer's face, an effect that would be lost entirely if the books were filed half an alphabet apart. And how strict are you prepared to be? Would *A Month in the Country* go under A or M? And *The Pickwick Papers*, T or P? These are all questions that need to be answered before you

71

start hauling your books from the shelves and piling them on the floor.

Alphabetical by author

Perhaps a more logical approach than alphabetical by title, gathering together books by the same author is the method favoured by most bookshops. That way nice matching hardback sets like the Everyman editions of P.G. Wodehouse can be displayed to their best effect, and Hilary Mantel's award-harvesting Tudor novels are surely best kept together. The key disadvantage of this method arises when you can't remember the author's name. Also, do you lump in all your fiction and non-fiction together or have separate

sections for both? Another possible pitfall is when the book is a collection or anthology containing work by many different writers – in these cases there's usually an editor credited somewhere on the cover and spine, but who remembers the name of the person who put together that anthology of uplifting poetry you like or that short-story collection by up-and-coming writers? Are you truly prepared to have your soul sapped and your neck cricked by passing along all your shelves in search of the book you're after because the compiler's name escapes you?

By genre

There is much to be said for arranging your books in sections defined by genre, but it's a task that feels at once like a job permanently half-done and impossible to complete. Let's say you divide your books into fiction and non-fiction ... what then? Do you alphabetise them by title or author? Or do you start introducing subcategories within genres? Fiction could be home to novels, novellas, poetry and short stories. Then there's translated fiction, literary fiction, science fiction, romantic fiction, fiction divided by century or literary movement, fiction divided by author nationality. The possibilities are even more labyrinthine in non-fiction: imagine the number of subcategories you could find yourself disappearing into in history alone: eras, topics, continents, countries, decades, social history vs political history vs military history, not to mention the dilemma of where to put books with attributes suiting several of your subdivisions. It's not an impossible notion that you'd end up finding each individual book its own individual category, placing you firmly back where you started with a random bunch of jumbled books.

Susan Sontag arranged her books this way, subdividing her fiction by language and chronology. 'The *Beowulf* to Virginia Woolf principle', she called it. James Ellroy also favours this method. 'I separate the

books into fiction and non-fiction and keep them rigorously alphabetised,' he says. 'Spines out, always. Dust jackets encased in plastic sheaths,' which seems to go a bit far but hey-ho.

By size

Aesthetically speaking, there is a decent argument for arranging your books in order of size. It's a system that gives a room a sense of order and neatness that's more pleasing to the eye than ranks of books in jagged rows. Indeed, one of the earliest records we have of books being stored on home bookshelves displayed them by size.

By the time of his death in 1703, Samuel Pepys' library ran to 3000 volumes. Exactly 3000. That's how he wanted it, that's how he liked it: 3000 books, no more, no less. Pepys wasn't just numerically meticulous either, he gave his library a level of attention to detail that has been rarely matched before or since. He had his books specially bound with gilt lettering on the sides so that every volume of roughly the same size became a uniform size on his shelves. He commissioned twelve large and ornate bookcases on which to store them and he filed the books on those shelves in size order beginning with the smallest. Not only that, each book was given a number, also inscribed in gilt, and recorded in a special ledger, number one being the smallest and 3000 the largest.

He's not often credited as such but Samuel Pepys deserves recognition as one of the greatest bibliophiles of all time. He was an avid collector (until he reached the magic 3000) with a number of regular London booksellers, many of whom he patronised for a number of years. In November 1667 his diary noted that one of his favourite booksellers, Joshua Kirton, died 'of grief for his losses by the fire'. London's bookstalls were traditionally gathered in the churchyard of St Paul's Cathedral and, when their proprietors saw the Great Fire of 1666 approaching, they quickly moved their wares into the undercroft of the cathedral for safe keeping. Unfortunately, at the height of the fire the cathedral floor collapsed, destroying all the books and sending poor Joshua Kirton into penury and a swirling depression.

Pepys also commissioned some of the earliest bookcases ever made in Britain. His diary entry for 17 August 1667 reads, 'So took up my wife and home, there I to the office, and thence with Sympson the joyner home to put together the press he hath brought

me for my books this day, which pleases me exceedingly'. A few days later he couldn't hide his delight at his new shelves. 'And then comes Sympson to set up my other new presses for my books,' he gushed, 'and so he and I fell into the furnishing of my new closet. I think it will be as noble a closet as any man hath.'

It's a testament to 'Sympson the joyner' that today, more than 350 years after he built them, Samuel Pepys' bookshelves are still in use at Magdalene College, Cambridge.

Pepys was unquestionably happy with his decision to store his books in size order, but he had the advantage of acquiring a number of books with which he was satisfied and calling it a day. His cataloguing of his library with what effectively amounted to a database helped him cope with the obvious disadvantage of the system: if you didn't have an idea of how large the book you wanted was and how that size compared with the other books on the shelves, a cat would have had a better chance of surviving in hell before you'd located the volume you were after. (Bill Clinton, incidentally, is another book cataloguer. According to Hillary Clinton's memoir *What Happened*, her husband carefully enters any new books added to his personal library into a computerised database.)

Those of us without the means to commission bookcases sturdy enough to survive almost half a millennium and have our books bound in matching, numbered leather covers would probably struggle a bit with storing by size. If books were uniform widths it would be a bit more straightforward, but what about those volumes that are wider than they are tall? Where do they go? In height order it would mean you'd have one book in the middle of the shelf sticking right out like a coach in a car park. You know that, whenever you stood and admired your shelves, this one odd-shaped book is the only thing you'd see protruding from the ranks like a literary hernia. The subsequent anguish would surely not be worth it. Put it at the end of the shelf? Then the whole thing would be out of height order. Mayhem would prevail. You'd have to start taking a tape measure into Waterstones and that would only mark you out as some kind of weirdo.

By colour

Certainly superficially the most pleasing method of filing books is by colour. Red books, blue books, green books: you could practically turn your shelves into a rainbow. This is a system that would suit, for example, the Penguin Classics and Modern Classics series

perfectly, lending a distinguished and classy air to the black and the white sections of your shelves. The pitfalls are many, however: the jumble of sizes, the mishmash of genres, and what about books whose spines contain many colours, or even just two in equal measure? What about books with, say, white spines on which title and author are displayed in large, thick red lettering? Where would they go? It's a system fraught with pitfalls. Recently the novelist Ayelet Waldman was dismayed to find that her husband had rearranged the books on the shelves of the family's summer home to be colour-coordinated, a move she considered particularly odd as both their children happen to be colour-blind. She now spends most summers buying second copies of books already on the shelves because she can't find anything. 'A tip for book-jacket designers looking to stand out,' she said. 'There are very few purple book jackets out there. Black, on the other hand, is sadly overused.'

By publisher

On first consideration this seems like an unnecessarily recondite method of categorisation, one that would be favoured only by those working in the industry as a way of celebrating their own publications and isolating those of rivals or sources of grudges. Yet there is a method to this apparent shelf madness. Consider the aforementioned Penguin Classics, for example, which look especially elegant when all lined up together. French publishers such as Gallimard produce books with classy white spines, black lettering and red numbers, and there is an increasing number of UK independent presses who produce books of a similar style and template: Persephone Books revive classic and forgotten titles written by women and publish them in exquisite matching grey hardback dust jackets, while Peirene Press produces a range of fiction in translation with a template cover. Not all publishers have a uniform visual style, however, meaning that most books

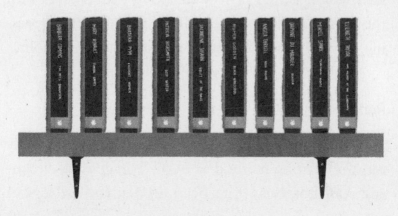

on your shelves if arranged by publisher will effectively just be placed at random. And all this ignores the fact that remembering the colours of one book's spine is a pretty niche ability, let alone hundreds of the things.

In order of purchase

An obscure filing method, for sure, but one that would serve as a telling chronology of a literary life. It's a straightforward methodology too: every new book just gets added to the shelf without the worry of alphabets or genres. The main drawback is in remembering which order you acquired your existing library, but you wouldn't need to be forensically dating paper or anything – an approximation would suffice. Imagine how satisfying it would be to walk along your shelves with the sensation that you're walking through time, passing through your own story measured out in books.

Randomly

Probably the easiest, least stressful and ultimately most rewarding method of book storage is to categorise your library as if it's been fired at the shelves out of a giant cannon. It's a particularly straightforward system for people who move house regularly: you can unload boxes of books onto the shelves in any order you please since there is no order. Yes, it'll be harder to locate specific books, but imagine the pleasure of browsing, of stumbling across books you've not read or even thought about for years because your eye is actually seeing each one rather than skimming over books in their rigid, classified places. The random system is a delightful disorder. If disorder is your thing, this is the system for you. Ditto: laziness.

'A good book is the best of friends,
the same today and forever.'

Martin Tupper

Ten rejected titles
for great books

It's a standard presence on most bookshelves belonging to people who consider themselves well read and is nominated more than most books as the Great American Novel itself, but would *The Great Gatsby* have secured its foothold in the literary canon if it had gone by any of these other titles that were under consideration by F. Scott Fitzgerald: *The High-Bouncing Lover? Under the Red, White and Blue? Trimalchio in West Egg? Gold-Hatted Gatsby? Among Ash-Heaps and Millionaires?*

Here are some other examples of books that have become standard titles in a personal library but whose spines might have looked quite different had they gone with their original monikers.

Shelf Respect

Strangers From Within (*Lord of the Flies*)

The Dead Un-Dead (*Dracula*)

Catch-11 (*Catch-22*)

The House of the Faith (*Brideshead Revisited*)

Tomorrow is Another Day (*Gone With the Wind*)

The Last Man in Europe (*Nineteen Eighty-Four*)

They Don't Build Statues to Businessmen (*The Valley of the Dolls*)

I Have Committed Fornication But That Was in Another Country (*A Farewell to Arms*)

All's Well That Ends Well (*War and Peace*)

First Impressions (*Pride and Prejudice*)

'What better occupation, really, than to spend the evening at the fireside with a book, with the wind beating on the windows and the lamp burning bright.'

Gustave Flaubert

A lender or borrower be?

What are the most stressful moments that life can throw at you? Bereavement? The break-up of a relationship? Losing your job? Well, yes, they're certainly up there, but how do they compare with the anxiety induced by the lending and borrowing of books? Hmm?

Take this example. You've embarked on a new romance. Things are looking promising. They're a keen reader too for a kick-off, but you're not getting carried away just yet. See how things go, no need to rush into anything. Then one day you're out on a date and watch your paramour reach into their bag and pull out a book. They hold it up, looking at you with a combination of enthusiasm and hope.

'This is that book I was telling you about,' they say. 'You know, my favourite one of all time.'

Your stomach goes cold: you know what's coming.

'Here, borrow it,' they say, holding the well-thumbed volume out towards you. 'I'd love to know what you think.'

You work like the proverbial Trojan so as not to betray the emotional convulsions that follow. Later, at home, you take it out and flip it over, reading the blurb on the back, still feeling the glow of eagerness with which it was handed to you. You place it on the table and look at it for a while; the slight curvature of the cracked spine, the furred page corners, the creases ploughed into the covers, all the signs of a book well loved and frequently read. There's a terrible thought swirling round your head: what if I don't like it? And have I really earned the right to read this? I mean, look at it, this is clearly more than just a book, it's a piece of a personality, a part of their very soul.

On the other side of the exchange, they watched you walk away carrying this small slab of themselves, this insight into what makes them the joyous, warm human being you've identified them to be. The excitement with which they pressed the book on you barely an hour earlier is mutating quickly into cold, hard fear. What if you don't like it? What if this book – their all-time favourite, the one they'd read countless times and loved like a family member – turned out to be not really your kind of thing? In the blushing early bloom of a relationship, when both parties rejoice in the repeated happy collisions of compatibility, this possibility hadn't even occurred to them until now, when it's too late. A vast fissure of self-doubt opens beneath them: this was, after all, more than a book, it was a piece of a personality, a part of their very soul.

Imagine the tension that follows. The book's there on your bedside table, pulsating with fears and doubts that are almost audible, keeping you awake until the milky light of dawn begins to seep around the curtains. Meanwhile they're awake too, the gap on their shelf yawning at them where the book normally lives, a tiny space that's transformed into a gaping chasm of self-doubt and crippling anxiety. In the days that follow there are cheery texts back and forth, studiously avoiding the subject of The Book. Your next date is dotted with slightly awkward silences, both of you knowing that the subject is lurking and each of you desperate to avoid blurting out something to do with a volume that by this stage might as well have been *The Elephant in the Room* by Dread McClench. You go and see a film together that, wouldn't you know it, features a scene where one of the characters lends a book to another, and in order to avoid catching the other's eye you both stare at the screen so hard you almost drill four little holes in it. Your hand spasms with anxiety, a hand that's holding the cardboard carton of popcorn, causing a sudden and catastrophic fountain of confectionary that covers both your laps.

That night, back at home, you realise you can't put it off any longer. You reach over to your bedside table, pick up the book, open it to the first page of the first chapter, sigh heavily, and start reading ...

Terrifying, isn't it? Imagine adding that kind of pressure to those early forays into mutual attraction: meeting the parents would be a cinch by comparison even if the parents turned out to be, say, the Putins. OK, that's a pretty extreme example but many are the pitfalls that go with the lending and borrowing of books, and we all need to be aware of even the worst-case scenarios. On the face of it, it should be the most straightforward and delightful thing in the world: you love a particular book and it strikes you that your friend/partner/colleague seems just the kind of person who would enjoy it too. You hand them the book, they go away and read it, return it to you agreeing that it is, indeed, a towering work of genius containing revealing insights into the human condition, brightening briefly but fundamentally our doomed existence on this spinning space rock, and reassuring you both that the other is confirmed as a splendid example of the best of humanity. Sometimes it works like that. It really does. Whether as a borrower or a lender, however, you have to ask yourself if such a positive outcome is really worth all the anxiety it involves.

This sort of lending and borrowing of books is a hell of a risk. For one thing, how long is reasonable for you to keep a book that someone's lent to you? Many of us have a teetering to-be-read pile that never seems to diminish no matter how much we read and, while the one you've borrowed does on the face of it look like the kind of book you'd enjoy very much, there's still that novel you've been dying to tear into, and that rigorous analysis of current affairs you really need to tackle while the subject is still at the forefront of the news. You can't give the book back without reading it – that would be rude – but equally you can't just hang on to it for as long as you like. Similarly, if you're the lender, how long is reasonable for the lendee to hang on to it before you begin getting a bit jumpy? There is no statute of limitations on borrowing a book, but what constitutes a decent length of time to allow before broaching the subject?

And what happens if you never get your book back? In the US between the wars this was such a heady issue that even in the catastrophic aftermath of the Wall Street Crash it was making the news. In December 1930 an organisation called the US Book Publishers' Research Institute announced a nationwide competition to devise a word for the person who comes to your house, peruses your shelves, borrows a book and then never returns it. Why this lexicographical vacancy was deemed serious enough to need filling at this particular time is a mystery: maybe the ravages of the Great Depression were seeing people borrowing books only to then try and sell them from a suitcase on a street corner. Either way, a trio of judges was appointed and tasked with sifting through a deluge of inventive neologisms – book-weevil, bibliosnitch, perusite, bogswoggler, bookibitzer and bookbummer were among the leading candidates – before selecting the winner: Paul W. Stoddard, an English teacher at Bulkeley High School in Hartford, Connecticut, who

'Dreams, books, are each a world; and
   books, we know,
Are a substantial world, both pure and
   good:
Round these, with tendrils strong as flesh
   and blood,
Our pastime and our happiness will grow.'

William Wordsworth

came up with 'booksneaf'. Mr Stoddard's prize was a selection of fifty books but booksneaf doesn't seem to have caught on. At least not yet.

Something else that makes borrowing a book an experience riddled with anxiety is the need to return it in the same condition it was in when you received it. Now, there are hundreds, maybe thousands of books in your home, none of which have ever been assailed by tea, coffee, red wine, curry, ketchup or blood, but if any of them were destined for such a fate then you know for certain that out of all the books in the place it's going to be the one you borrowed from nice Janice in HR. No matter how hard you try to keep a borrowed book pristine, practically treating it like an illuminated medieval manuscript to the extent of putting on white cotton gloves every time you handle it, the Law of Sod dictates that something bad will happen, whether it be half a pan of bolognese sauce or an unexpected sneeze (or, worse, a combination of the two).

What if it's your book that a borrower returns christened with gravy or with puckered pages smelling faintly of Sancerre? A lot depends of course on your attitude to books in the first place: whether you like them to remain as blemish-free as the day they rolled off the press with that heady sharp tang of fresh ink or whether you're happy for your books to look lived in. If it's the latter then lending books is probably a safe thing to do. If the former is more your style, well, perhaps lending isn't for you.

The borrower's attitude to damage – major or minor – will also play its part here. An apology at least is required, and if the damage is bad enough hopefully they'll pony up a replacement copy without fuss, but as long as they're up front about it then everyone wins. There's a possibly apocryphal story about Winston Churchill once lending a book to someone only to find when it was returned there were grease spots all through the pages. Irked as much by how the borrower hadn't mentioned the damage as the stains themselves, Churchill stuck a sardine in an envelope and sent it to them accompanied by a note saying, 'You forgot your bookmark.'

For all its admirable intentions, the act of lending a book to someone is riddled with these anxieties and potential pitfalls, for which there are plenty of historic precedents. In Zurich in 1922, for example, a man who'd lent a book 'worth eight shillings' to a friend and never had it returned went as far as taking his pal to court in an effort to retrieve his book. Not only did the magistrate order the borrower to return the book, he slapped him with a hefty fine and sent him to prison for two days, commenting, 'A book is a family utensil like furniture and is necessary for the welfare of the family'.

A man named Jacques Bessner from the Alsace region of France was prosecuted in 1859 under the region's recently introduced Hawkers' Act and fined 50 francs for lending a book to a neighbour without first obtaining an official stamp granting him permission to do so. In possibly the most extreme case – one that might put you off lending books for ever – in 1793 a Scottish lawyer and political radical named Thomas Muir lent his copy of Thomas Paine's *Rights of Man* to some friends in Paisley, an act that saw him charged with sedition and – get this – transported to Australia for fourteen years.

All this is grist to the mill of the reluctant lender – 'I'd like nothing more than to let you borrow it but I don't have the official stamp and I can't risk prison, not with my allergies' – but these martyrs to the temporary dissemination of literature serve only to illustrate why we still do it despite the risks. It's that heady mix of hope and delicious tension contained in the moment when we've accepted the returned book and asked what the borrower thought. In that instant hangs the potential deflation of 'I couldn't really get into it, to be honest,' or worse, the unconvincing, not-meeting-your-eye outright fib: 'Yeah, it was all right, I enjoyed it.'

Best of all, of course, is the moment that makes all the stress and anxiety worthwhile: when they bring the book back, hold it up, rap its cover with their knuckles and say, 'Wow. Amazing. I loved it.'

For all the delight – and relief – of that moment, at the same time we can all identify with Elizabeth Miller of Aylesbury who, in the summer of 1899, was sentenced at the local petty sessions to fourteen days in prison for using obscene language in a public place.

'The defendant made a statement about lending a book to Mrs Eliza Cook who returned it in a dilapi-dated condition,' the trial transcript records. 'This is what caused her to use bad language.'

And they call that justice.

Ten great quotes about books and reading

'Do not read, as children do, to amuse yourself, or like the ambitious, for the purpose of instruction. No, read in order to live.'

Gustave Flaubert

'When I have a little money, I buy books; and if I have any left, I buy food and clothes.'

Desiderius Erasmus

'It is a great thing to start life with a small number of really good books which are your very own.'

Arthur Conan Doyle

Shelf Respect

'My Best Friend is a person who will give me a book I have not read.'

Abraham Lincoln

'A house without books is like a room without windows.'

Horace Mann

'The love of learning, the sequestered nooks,
And all the sweet serenity of books.'

Henry Wadsworth Longfellow

'The worst thing about new books is that they keep us from reading the old ones.'

Joseph Joubert

'Books are the treasured wealth of the world and the fit inheritance of generations and nations.'

Henry David Thoreau

Ten great quotes about books and reading

'For books are not absolutely dead things, but do contain a potency of life in them to be as active as that soul was whose progeny they are; nay, they do preserve as in a vial the purest efficacy and extraction of that living intellect that bred them.'

John Milton

'I know every book of mine by its smell, and I have but to put my nose between the pages to be reminded of all sorts of things.'

George Gissing

Strange things found in books

M any of us will have had the delightful experience of opening a second-hand volume we've bought and finding inside evidence of previous ownership. The older the book, the more common this is and the more exciting. There are the basic inkings of a previous owner's name, occasional elaborate pasted bookplates with engravings of classical scenes and the words *Ex Libris*, and often a detailed inscription revealing your book was once a treasured gift. Rarer still, we might find a pressed flower or an old photograph or letter, possibly used as a bookmark, possibly deliberately hidden. These discoveries serve only to enhance the enjoyment of our bibliophilia, the evidence and realisation that every book has a story separate from the one on its pages and that, for all our often jealously guarded protection of our own books, we are just their temporary custodians. Many, if not most, of them will outlast us and move on to somebody else who'll treasure them as much as we did and wonder about their previous owner.

Not everything found inside a book is an immediate cause of delight, however. In 1953, for example, librarians at the British Museum were startled to find a selection of eighteenth-century condoms (unused) made from animal membrane with silk ribbons at the open end to secure them in place. They were, perhaps appropriately, tucked inside a copy of *A Guide To Health, Beauty, Riches and Honour* by Francis Grose, published in 1783. The Georgians were liberated people in many ways but it's unlikely their prophylactics would have been, say, laid out and displayed on a dressing table in an agreeably symmetrical pattern, so it's probably understandable that the ones found by the librarians would have been secreted between the pages of a book. Their continued presence there more than two centuries on might suggest their owner had forgotten which book they were in, however, despite the faint clue in the title he or she selected as their repository. Imagine them getting frisky in the bedchamber one night, pausing to take the necessary precautions and killing the moment by ending up frenziedly pulling books from shelves and flicking through the pages. Who knows, there may even be a decent-sized spinney of family trees in the world today as a result of those particular items avoiding discovery all those years ago.

Ancient contraceptives are not the strangest things to have turned up inside a book either. In May 2019 Twitter lit up with librarians reporting some of the curious items they'd discovered tucked, stuffed or secreted inside books during the course of their duties. These included a circular saw blade, a slice of processed cheese, a rasher of bacon, a banana, a leg of fried chicken (chewed), a Polaroid of a cat in a leather mask, a 78" disc of *Frosty the Snowman*, a baby carrot and the eight of hearts.

'Me, poor man, my library was
dukedom large enough.'

William Shakespeare, *The Tempest*

A dozen books read on screen in films

Beyond Good and Evil by Friedrich Nietzsche, read by Otto West (Kevin Kline) in *A Fish Called Wanda*

The Bell Jar by Sylvia Plath, read by Mallory Knox (Juliette Lewis) in *Natural Born Killers*

The Hollow Men by T.S. Eliot, read by Colonel Kurtz (Marlon Brando) in *Apocalypse Now*

Love in the Time of Cholera by Gabriel García Márquez, read by Sarah Thomas (Kate Beckinsale) in *Serendipity*

A dozen books read on screen in films

The Icarus Agenda by Robert Ludlum, read by Harry Burns (Billy Crystal) in *When Harry Met Sally*

Captain Corelli's Mandolin by Louis de Bernières, read by William Thacker (Hugh Grant) in *Notting Hill*

Modesty Blaise by Peter O'Donnell, read by Vincent Vega (John Travolta) in *Pulp Fiction*

The Catcher in the Rye by J.D. Salinger, read by Wendy Torrance (Shelley Duvall) in *The Shining*

The Adventures of Tom Sawyer by Mark Twain, read by George Bailey (James Stewart) in *It's a Wonderful Life*

Mrs Dalloway by Virginia Woolf, read by Laura Brown (Julianne Moore) in *The Hours*

A Connecticut Yankee in King Arthur's Court by Mark Twain, read by Alex Price (Jenny Agutter) in *An American Werewolf in London*

The Cat in the Hat by Dr Seuss, read by Morticia Addams (Anjelica Huston) in *Addams Family Values*

'A book is a garden, an orchard, a
storehouse, a party, a company by the way,
a counsellor, a multitude of counsellors.'

Charles Baudelaire

Death by bookcase

The French composer Charles-Valentin Alkan is said to have died as a result of a bookcase toppling over and falling on him as he reached for a volume on a high shelf in 1888 at the age of seventy-four.

In 2010 the renowned playwright Tom Stoppard announced that if he could choose a way to shuffle off this mortal coil, it would be a similar death by bookcase.

'It would be a good way to go,' he said. 'You went when you were in a good frame of mind and you were doing something pleasant and interesting. A lot of people would say, "I would rather have a heart attack at the height of sexual passion," but on the whole, I would prefer to be killed by a bookcase.'

'No story is the same to us after a lapse of time; or rather we who read it are no longer the same interpreters.'

George Eliot

Fifteen books from the personal library of Marilyn Monroe

The Fall by Albert Camus

The Boston Cooking-School Cook Book by Fannie Merritt-Farmer

Ulysses by James Joyce

On the Road by Jack Kerouac

The Little Engine That Could by Watty Piper (containing pencil scrawls possibly in a young Monroe's own hand)

Fifteen books from the personal library of Marilyn Monroe

A Farewell to Arms by Ernest Hemingway

The Portable Walt Whitman

Two Plays: Peace And Lysistrata by Aristophanes

Madame Bovary by Gustave Flaubert

Portrait of the Artist as a Young Dog by Dylan Thomas

A Shropshire Lad by A.E. Housman

Das Kapital by Karl Marx

The Brothers Karamazov by Fyodor Dostoevsky

The Ballad of the Sad Cafe by Carson McCullers

'Nowhere is the modern litter of knick-knacks and photographs more inappropriate than in the library. The tables should be large, substantial, and clear of everything but lamps, books and papers – one table at least being given over to the filing of books and newspapers. The library writing-table is seldom large enough, or sufficiently free from odds and ends in the shape of photograph-frames, silver boxes, and flower-vases, to give free play to the elbows.'

Edith Wharton

'The harmless and delicious fever': How bibliophilic are you?

It's a fair assumption that you're holding this book because you or someone close to you recognises your love of the written word. In all likelihood you have at least one wall of shelves covered in books and there are probably books on your coffee table, bedside table and in your bathroom – some read, some half-read and the rest waiting to be read. We all feel that excitement of picking up a new book, running our fingertips over the cover, a faint tingle in our stomachs at the prospect of immersing ourselves in its contents. We might read it on the sofa, in bed, on the way to work, on holiday, in a cafe or in the pub with a quiet drink, all scenarios of precious intimacy, of 'me time'.

Bibliophiles have been under a bit of pressure in recent years. In the pacy, connected world we live in it can be increasingly difficult to isolate ourselves with a book for a significant length of time. The phone in our pocket demands we check our WhatsApps and emails, the news headlines and weather, the train times for that trip this weekend. We're wired to the world in a way we've never been before, rendering time to read even more valuable by its scarcity as much as its contribution to our mental wellness. The author Amy Tan even says she often mulls over committing a minor crime resulting in three to six months in prison purely in order to get stuck into some undistracted reading.

Those of us who love the physical aspect of books as much as their contents – the way they look, the way they feel, the way they take up a tangible space in our lives and on our shelves – have also come through the digital wars, years of being told the printed book was obsolete, it was dying, that digital was the future, that the book was somehow an inferior object purely because you couldn't plug it in.

Thankfully e-readers have settled into a healthy co-existence with physical books and it no longer feels necessary for one to justify itself or exclude the other.

Indeed, the publishing industry seems to have been jolted out of a complacency that had resulted in dull-looking, poorly produced volumes and remembered what makes physical books special: their attraction as tangible objects. We're reading better-quality books now in terms of design, layout and format. So much so that it's now cool again to be a bibliophile and we are safe in the knowledge that we are maintaining a noble and ancient tradition.

In 1843 the French author and librarian Charles Nodier set out three main categories he'd identified in book lovers:

'The bibliophile is a man gifted with some *esprit* and some taste who takes pleasure in works of genius, imagination and feeling. He likes that mute conversation of great minds which requires no reciprocity, which he may commence where he pleases, drop without rudeness, and resume without importunity. The bibliophile of our times is the *savant*, the literary man, the artist, and petty landowner of moderate income who makes up, by an intercourse with books, for the insipidity of his intercourse with man and whom a harmless taste consoles more or less for the falseness of our other affections.

117

'The bibliomane. Where the bibliophile knows how to select books; the bibliomane heaps them up. The bibliophile adds book to book after subjecting them to all the investigations of his senses and intellects; the bibliomane heaps books together without looking at them. The bibliophile appreciates a book; the bibliomane weighs and measures it. The bibliophile proceeds with a lens and the bibliomane with a yard: I know some who reckon the riches of their library by the square foot. The harmless and delicious fever of the bibliophile is in the bibliomane an acute disease carried unto delirium.

'The bouquiniste, properly so called, is usually an old rentier, a professor who has served his time or a man of letters out of fashion, who has sustained a taste for books but not circumstances easy enough to buy them. This amateur is perpetually searching for those precious old books which capricious chance may, peradventure, have hidden in the dust of a stall.'

So, what kind of bibliophile are you? What fires your acquisition of books? Are you a hoarder, reckoning the riches of your library by the square foot? Or are you turning to books to console more or less for the falseness of our other affections? Perhaps you just like a good story, well told and presented in a format that makes you want to hang on to it and keep it on your shelf for the rest of your days, part of a collection that anchors you to the world and the wonders it contains?

It was probably A. Edward Newton who summed it up best in his 1921 memoir *A Magnificent Farce, And Other Diversions of a Book Collector* in which he writes, 'it is my pleasure to buy more books than I can read. Who was it who said, "I hold the buying of more books than one can peradventure read, as nothing less than the soul's reaching towards infinity; which is the only thing that raises us above the beasts that perish"? Whoever it was, I agree with him.'

And so say all of us.

'Reading is that fruitful miracle of a communication in the midst of solitude.'

Marcel Proust

Some notable bibliophiles

For most of us, constraints of space and cash are the key limiters of our literary acquisition. Although we might convince ourselves that rationality and discernment are the drivers of our bookish life, deep down we know that if we were granted boundless space and unlimited resources we would end up with thousands upon thousands of books.

How many can we read in a single lifetime? Let's assume that we make it to eighty before shuffling off this mortal coil. If we read a book every single day from the age of eighteen to our eightieth birthday – every day including Christmas Day, bank holidays, hangover days, busy days at work, wedding days, birthdays – a whole book a day no exceptions, then allowing for leap years that would be 24,837 books. Let's pare that down a bit and assume we get through an average of a book a week during our adult lives, still a tall-ish order but feasible. That comes to 3536 books. Let's say we keep them all and put them on bookcases consisting of six shelves, with each shelf holding thirty books. An adult lifetime's reading at a rate of one book a week would by that calculation fit onto twenty bookcases, which doesn't actually sound a massive amount for a lifetime's reading, does it? It sounds even less when you think about some of the more extreme collectors who've amassed some of history's biggest libraries.

Richard de Bury, a noted fourteenth-century bibliophile who wrote the first book dedicated to the subject of collecting books, was forced to 'climb over his books to reach his bed', while Charles van Hulthem was a Belgian bibliophile who lived at the turn of the nineteenth century. His personal library ran to an estimated 32,000 books divided between a house in Brussels and one in Ghent. So great was the risk of fire among all that paper, he allowed no naked flame to be displayed in either house and kept warm when required by draping manuscripts over himself. On his death in 1832 his collection became the foundation of the National Library of Belgium.

*

In the eighteenth century the London barrister and book collector Thomas Rawlinson, 'who gathered books much as a squirrel gathers nuts', had so many books he was eventually forced to sleep in the draughty hallway of his house in Gray's Inn. The satirist Joseph Addison is said to have based his character Tom Folio, 'a learned fool', on Rawlinson.

In 1906 Wolverhampton police found George Griffiths dead in his run-down lodgings at the heart of the town's slums. It appeared that Griffiths – an ironworker who lived alone – had starved to death, but when the officers investigated the contents of his room they found his death had certainly not occurred through poverty: bank books showed him to be several hundred pounds in credit and there were seven watches and a number of gold sovereigns in a box under his bed. Most notable, however, were the 2000 rare and valuable books stacked in piles around the room.

'He never had visitors. He lived with his books and used to say nobody need be lonely if they had books,' said the landlady of Lionel Treherne of Westhill Road, Brighton, after his death in 1923 at the age of

WHITE TEETH ZADIE SMITH

M.R. JAMES

A THIN GHOST AND OTHERS

THE GIRL WITH THE DRAGON TATTOO

STIEG LARSSON

Shakespeare's Sonnets

A TALE OF TWO CITIES

THE GIRL ON THE TRAIN
PAULA HAWKINS

THE PORTRAIT OF A LADY

HILARY MANTEL WOLF HALL

ORANGES ARE NOT THE ONLY FRUIT
JEANETTE WINTERSON

HENRY JAMES

William Finnegan Barbarian Days A Surfing Life

fifty-four, adding 'he even denied himself food to buy more books'. Treherne was well known around the Sussex town for his eccentricities, not least how at the height of summer he would be seen out wearing two overcoats, carrying a mackintosh over his arm and holding an umbrella unfurled over his head. Known affectionately as 'the Colonel', he would frequent Brighton's second-hand bookshops, and when he died there were an estimated 15,000 volumes piled floor to ceiling in his attic room, leaving barely enough space to move between the door and the bed. After they were removed the books were reckoned to have a combined weight of two tons. Treherne lived on dry bread and cocoa and rarely slept, often pacing the streets at night, composing poetry.

In Los Angeles in January 1983, when retired postal worker Michael Hurley died at his home at the age of seventy-seven, he left behind an astonishing literary legacy. Crammed into his modest two-bedroom house was a collection of books estimated at more than 35,000 volumes, some of them so rare it made Hurley – who never earned more than $25,000 in a year – one of the world's leading collectors of antiquarian books.

Iowa-born Hurley had hitchhiked to California in 1930 at the start of the Great Depression (according to friends once he arrived in Los Angeles he never left the city again, not even for a day) and began his collection four years later. In half a century of book collecting he acquired among other things a 1632 Second Folio of the *Complete Works of Shakespeare*, a first edition of Boswell's *Life of Samuel Johnson*, a signed first edition of Bram Stoker's *Dracula*, a first edition of *The Waste Land* by T.S. Eliot and an edition of *Winnie-the-Pooh* signed by both A.A. Milne and illustrator E.H. Shepard – one of only twenty such vellum-bound editions ever produced. He left no will; the collection was sold off by the local authorities.

According to his biographer, the early-nineteenth-century bibliophile Sir Thomas Phillipps' collection of 50,000 books and 60,000 manuscripts cost him 'perhaps between two hundred thousand and a quarter of a million pounds, altogether four or five thousand pounds a year, while accessions came in at the rate of forty or fifty a week'. He would walk into bookshops and buy their entire stock; similarly at auctions he would buy entire lots, usually outbidding his only serious rival for such literary prizes – the British Museum – in the nation's salerooms. Phillipps' Worcestershire stately home comprised twenty rooms, of which sixteen were given over to books. When for security reasons he decided to move his collection to his house at Cheltenham, the process took 105 carts and lasted eight months. His stated aim was to own a copy of every book ever published, and his relentless collecting saw him fall into heavy debt in his later years. After the death of his wife in 1837 he advertised an appeal to 'any lady with £50,000; I am available at that price'.

By the time Stephen Blumberg was arrested at his Minnesota home in the early hours of 20 March 1990, he had stolen nearly 24,000 rare and valuable books from more than 250 museums, universities and institutions in forty-five US states and two Canadian provinces. The value of Blumberg's literary booty was pegged at $5,300,000. His defence was that he was saving the precious volumes for the nation as he believed the government was planning to revoke the public's right to access rare and beautiful books. He served four and a half years in prison and was hit with a $200,000 fine. His arrest came after his erstwhile friend Kenneth J. Rhodes turned him in in return for a $56,000 bounty.

In the light of these extraordinary hoarders and collectors, our own groaning bookshelves suddenly don't seem quite so excessive. Among other things, that means it's absolutely fine to go and ahead and check out all those books you've had sitting for ages in your cyber-shopping baskets on retail sites across the internet. Go on, honestly, it's fine. If you do decide to take a more nefarious route to literary acquisition, however, be sure not to tell your friend Kenneth. He'll only dob you in to the peelers in return for a few measly quid.

Incidentally, if you're wondering about the bookmarks you'd need to facilitate massive collections like these, you may be interested to know that the largest collection of bookmarks in the world is believed to belong to Frank Divendal of Alkmaar in the Netherlands who, since he began his collection in 1982, has amassed somewhere north of 120,000. That means that if you assign one bookmark to every book you read in a lifetime at the rate of one a week, Frank Divendal has enough bookmarks to last thirty-four lifetimes.

'Books, books, books!
    I had found the secret of a garret room
Piled high with cases in my father's name;
Piled high, packed large, where, creeping in
    and out
Among the giant fossils of my past,
Like some small nimble mouse between the
    ribs
Of a mastodon, I nibbled here and there
At this or that box, pulling through the gap,
In heats of terror, haste, victorious joy,
The first book first. And how I felt it beat
Under my pillow, in the morning's dark,
An hour before the sun would let me read!
My books!'

                Elizabeth Barrett Browning

J.K. Rowling's favourite childhood reading

The Little White Horse by Elizabeth Goudge

Little Women by Louisa May Alcott

Manxmouse by Paul Gallico

Black Beauty by Anna Sewell

Anything by Noel Streatfeild

Anything by E. Nesbit

The merging of the book collections

There are few more exciting times in life than moving in with a romantic partner. There's the thrill that you're going to be able to spend all that 'normal' time with them, taking turns to cook, doing the weekly shop together, dividing up wardrobe and cupboard space and slumping on the sofa in the evenings while scrolling listlessly through Netflix. Never does the drudgery of everyday life – household chores, sorting out bills – feel quite so exhilarating as when you first launch your voyage of cohabitation.

For all the joyous romance, there are still potential obstacles waiting below the rainbow-glitter surface on which toes can painfully be stubbed. That novelty Goofy lamp looks adorable now, but how about when you've been looking at it every day for six months? Do those cushion covers really go with that armchair? And aren't we a little long in the tooth for those *He-Man and the Masters of the Universe* pillowcases? Yes, granted there should be an accompanying duvet cover but it only comes in a single size – why do you think that is?

Perhaps the most intimate part of the process is The Great Combination of the Books, the day you both stand together in front of the empty shelves and begin filling them with your collections. This is a rare part of your new home where your individual possessions will properly mingle and intertwine, throwing up both strong supporting evidence as to why you are so compatible and the odd hint that, as well as all those seemingly miraculous things you have in common, there are differences too.

Hopefully there shouldn't be too much argument about the book-filing system. Let's assume you've sorted that out before slicing through the packing tape on your respective boxes. If your partner insists their books be kept entirely separate from yours then loud alarm bells should ring; ditto if they suggest you write your individual names inside the covers of

132

your books 'so we know whose is who'. These are not good omens.

Passing over those particular get-the-hell-out-of-there-before-it's-too-late scenarios, let's move on to the books on the shelves. A good sign would be that you find plenty of doubles, books that you both own, but which do you keep? It's possible that you each have a different edition, which could look OK on the shelf next to each other as a reminder that, while you're both different, look, you're *still kinda the same* (dawwww!).

A possible drawback, especially when your editions are exact duplicates, is what to do with the extra one. The flush of love gushing through both your hearts says they should go, for this library is, like your relationship, for life and you'll only need one copy of any book for ever and ever from this day forwards. Whatever you do, don't say, 'Tell you what, why don't I put my doubles in this box and stick them in the loft?' Do not, under any circumstances, say this, even if you are convinced this is absolutely a lifelong commitment and are just pathologically averse to getting rid of books for any reason like any normal person. Innocent though your intentions might be, it's akin to announcing 'I'm not sure we're for keeps' and will not – repeat *not* – go down well. For the good of your eternal happiness, take it on the chin and offer to whack the doubles up on eBay or take them to the charity shop – both acts speaking of firm commitment, not to say undying love. After you've said that, make sure the box is well hidden when you put it in the shed or up in the eaves.

Once the books are on the shelves and you've both posted a picture online with the obligatory hashtags #newhome, #books, #morebooks, #truelove and #happiness, it's then that you begin to realise what a vital role those bookshelves and their contents are going to play in your relationship. In the early days in particular they will practically act as a barometer.

You can't really know a person until you see how they treat a book. It's only once you start into each other's literary tastes that your true natures will be revealed. Your delight that your love is sitting up in bed reading that hardback first edition you raved about and is absolutely loving it might be tempered when you see that, rather than using a bookmark to keep their place when the lights go off, they've tucked the front flap of the dust jacket between the pages. That's fine for the early part of the book – indeed, in these early days of cohabitation, it's completely adorable and you keep asking what bit they've got up to and isn't it great and isn't that character great and aren't they a fabulous writer – but if they get to the halfway point and are still using the front flap, then start using the back flap for the rest of the book, making the edges of the cover all puffy and tatty, your eager smile is, in cartoon terms, soon going to be replaced with a wavy line.

Similarly with paperbacks, what if you are a committed bookmark user but your partner favours turning down the corners of the pages or, worse, folding the page practically in half so the outside corner meets the spine? Or they plonk the book on the table or floor, open with pages facing down, ready to pick up and continue where they left off, leaving the front and back covers curling outwards for evermore? And what if it's you who – not even contemplating that someone else might not appreciate your belief that books are designed to be read and should be seen to have been read – is the unwitting cause of internal conniptions in your beloved?

As with all relationship issues, communication is the key. Don't let these bibliographic blunders fester, for then they will grow to epic proportions and become a major part of an argument artillery ready to be launched over no man's land during the Battle of Do We Really Need to Visit Your Parents *Every* Weekend. Only diplomacy can lead to disarmament, and early diplomacy is the best course.

It's either that or resign yourself to a lifetime of seeing your paperbacks springing open into the shape of a Christmas tree whenever they're removed from the shelf. Or feeling the bedroom temperature drop by a few degrees every time you fold the corner of a page into a dog's ear.

Ten prolific authors

Enid Blyton – 762 books

Barbara Cartland – 723 books

Ursula Bloom – 560 books

Isaac Asimov – 469 books

Georges Simenon – 425 books

Alexandre Dumas – 277 books

H.G. Wells – 114 books

P.G. Wodehouse – 71 books

Stephen King – 65 books

Donald Trump – 19 books

(Figures correct as of July 2019)

138

———————

'Some books are so familiar that reading them is like being home again.'

Louisa May Alcott

———————

Bookshelves that
made history

Bookshelves and bookcases don't tend to draw attention to themselves, generally being happy playing a supporting role to the volumes they embrace. The bookcase is a humble thing, shelf-effacing you might even say (sorry), quietly getting on with its job like a literary Atlas, holding up the world in the form of its literature, shepherding together books of different topics, designs and character, and keeping them together for as long as you need.

Rarely does the bookcase itself float noticeably on the surface of the great torrent of history. Its contents often define and even shape the course of history and science but the apparatus on which they rest just quietly gets on with things, never complaining, never boasting, always happy to be in the background. Occasionally, however, the bookcase does find itself at the forefront.

Perhaps the most historically resonant example is the bookcase at the Anne Frank House on Westermarkt in Amsterdam. 'Now our Secret Annex has truly become secret,' wrote Anne in her diary on 21 August 1942. 'Because so many houses are being searched for hidden bicycles Mr Kugler thought it would be better to have a bookcase built in front of the entrance to our hiding place. It swings out on its hinges and opens like a door. Mr Voskuijl did the carpentry work.' Johannes Voskuijl was the warehouse manager at the company run by Anne's father, and you can still see his handi-work when you visit the Anne Frank House today and pass through the secret entrance to the annex where the Frank and van Pels families hid for nearly two years before their fatal discovery in 1944. When Anne made that entry in her diary, the Franks had been living secretly in the annex for five weeks and it was clearly felt the entrance needed the extra security of a con-cealing bookcase. The scrapes and dings of more than half a century of tourists since the house opened to the public in 1960 meant that since 2013 the bookcase has been partially contained within a glass case, but the important thing is that it's still there – a valuable, tangible link to the horrors of the Holocaust.

Napoleon Bonaparte always liked to travel with books – his brother recalled that, even as a young artillery officer, Napoleon's books 'filled a trunk larger than the one containing his toiletries' – and by the time he became a continent-conquering emperor he needed more and more of them to hand for reasons of both reference and recreation. And so in 1808 Napoleon commissioned an extraordinary travelling library from his personal librarian to ensure his military campaigning didn't interfere with his reading. A thousand numbered, catalogued volumes were transported in specially made cases that opened out into ready-made shelving. He wanted his favourite classics, such as those by Homer and Plutarch, and works of history nearby for easy reference when on the road or on the battlefield, but there was plenty of leisure reading too. There were forty English novels including Laurence Sterne's *Tristam Shandy*, while the portable bookcases also contained volumes of Racine and Voltaire, the

Arabian Nights, Cook's *Voyages* and Goethe's sensational *Sorrows of Young Werther* (which, Napoleon once told its author, he'd read seven times). There were a few surprises too: Gresset's mock-epic poem *Vert-Vert* about a foul-mouthed parrot in a nunnery and – arguably Napoleon's all-time favourite – the works of the ancient Gaelic bard Ossian (now widely accepted as an eighteenth-century hoax). Napoleon's portable units are rare examples of bookcases that actually witnessed some of history's most important moments.

An unsung hero of the Second World War was Roberta 'Betty' de Mauduit. Born in Berwickshire in 1891 and raised in Minnesota, she met and married her husband, the aristocratic diplomat Henri de Mauduit, while working as a fashion buyer in Paris, then moving to his Breton chateau Bourblanc in 1925. In the early part of the war Bourblanc served as a hospital for French troops and housed hundreds of refugees who had fled Paris when the Germans arrived. Later, with Henri having slipped across the Channel to join de Gaulle in England, Betty began hiding downed British and American airmen between a double floor in the chateau while nearby fishing smacks prepared to spirit them away to England. All the while Betty kept up the pretence of personal neutrality. On one occasion she was even joined for lunch at Bourblanc by the chief engineer of Germany's coastal defences on a day when seventeen airmen were hiding in the house.

In June 1943 a Gestapo unit a hundred strong suddenly arrived to search the chateau and, while they didn't find the five airmen hiding there at the time, they arrested Betty anyway, keeping her in solitary confinement for more than a month on a diet of black bread and water. Moved to Ravensbrück concentration camp, she was beaten regularly with rubber flails and made to stand at attention outside in the freezing cold until she fainted. She never talked, never betrayed the airmen she'd helped to save. After being liberated she was driven to Paris and reunited with Henri, who had parachuted into France the day before and as a colonel was able to liberate his own chateau shortly afterwards.

For the last two years of the war Nazi officers and soldiers had been billeted at Bourblanc. Thankfully they weren't bibliophiles, as hidden among the volumes on the shelves was the guestbook Betty had kept containing the names, details and dates of all the soldiers who had been hidden at Bourblanc up to the day of Betty's arrest. Its discovery would have resulted in her immediate execution, but the bookshelves of Bourblanc refused to give up their secret.

When Oscar Wilde was imprisoned for two years in 1895 for gross indecency, one of the most daunting prospects he faced was a dearth of reading material. For the first three months of their sentences English prisoners were permitted only the Bible, a hymn book and a book of prayers. Straightaway Wilde wrote to the prison authorities, begging to be allowed a wider variety of reading matter but, with the grudging exception by the Reading Gaol governor that he be allowed a copy of Bunyan's *Pilgrim's Progress*, he was initially refused. He wrote in desperation to his friend the Liberal Member of Parliament R.B. Haldane, who subsequently visited and found a tearful Wilde asking him to pull a few strings and provide him with Flaubert's works at least.

'I said that the dedication by that author to his advocate, who had successfully defended Flaubert from a charge of indecent publication, made such a book as *Madame Bovary* unlikely to be sanctioned,' Haldane wrote in his memoir published in 1929. 'He laughed and became cheerful.'

Eventually the authorities relaxed a little, or just gave in to Wilde's stream of letters – 'The Library here contains no example of any of Thackeray's or Dickens's novels. I feel sure that a complete set of their works would be as great a boon to many amongst the other prisoners as it certainly would be to myself' – and the writer was allowed to keep up to twenty books from the prison library in his cell at any one time, which was enough to warrant a small bookcase. He thanked the prison governor for his bibliophilic kindness by later sending him an inscribed copy of *The Important of Being Earnest*. Wilde might not have been a great person to lend books to, however. He had a habit of tearing off the top corner of each page as he read, and eating it.

Perhaps the most moving example of historically significant bookshelves doesn't contain any books and dates back only to 1995. There's a glass panel in the ground at the centre of Bebelplatz in the heart of Berlin, and if you look down through it you'll see a perfectly white room containing perfectly white and empty floor-to-ceiling bookshelves. Installed by the Israeli artist Micha Ullman, there is space on the shelves for 20,000 books, the number estimated to have been burned on the same spot on 10 May 1933 by the Nazi-sympathising German Students' Union with the encouragement of the Nazi Party. The books were all by authors discredited by the Hitler regime – a literary list, which included the likes of Sigmund Freud, Karl Marx and Stefan Zweig, drawn up by a librarian named Wolfgang Herrmann. The books were taken from public libraries, academic institutions and private homes and immolated as organisers chanted how they were 'against decadence and moral decay' and 'for discipline and decency in the family and the nation'. It was a rainy night and the fire kept going out, meaning the fire brigade had to pour petrol onto the smouldering, sludgy mass of damp paper to keep the conflagration going.

More than a century earlier the German writer Heinrich Heine had written with remarkable prescience, *'Dort wo man Bücher verbrennt, verbrennt man auch am Ende Menschen'* – or 'Where books are burned, in the end people will also be burned.'

'For books are more than books,
they are the life, the very heart and
core of ages past, the reason why men
worked and died, the essence and
quintessence of their lives.'

Cicero

Great sliding bookcases

From classic horror to cartoons, melodrama to spoof, the sliding or revolving bookcase has been a popular on-screen device since the dawn of cinema. The first example of the bookcase-as-secret-entrance was in Ann Radcliffe's 1797 Gothic novel *The Italian* and from there it progressed until there was one in *Columbo*, one in *Midsomer Murders* and practically one a week in *Scooby Doo*. Here is some of the humble piece of movable joinery's finest work.

Batman

In the classic US series from the 1960s starring Adam West as Bruce Wayne and Burt Ward as Dick Grayson, access to the Batcave was via a pair of firemen's poles concealed behind a sliding bookcase in the study of

Wayne Manor. The mechanism was triggered by a switch hidden inside a bust of William Shakespeare, which caused the bookcase to slide back and reveal twin poles labelled 'Bruce' and 'Dick'. Somehow both men manage to change into their Batman and Robin costumes on the way down the poles.

Frasier

Niles Crane's apartment contains a sumptuous and well-stocked personal library. It also contains a sliding bookcase revealing a secret staircase to a landing on the floor above. According to Niles, the mechanism is activated by 'poking *Mrs Dalloway* on the bottom'.

Young Frankenstein

Mel Brooks' spoof of classic horror films wouldn't have been complete without a revolving bookcase at the heart of Castle Frankenstein and the heart of the story. Gene Wilder as Frederick Frankenstein and Teri Garr as his assistant Inga accidentally set off the rotating bookcase when Inga removes a candle from a holder, triggering the mechanism. There follows two minutes of mayhem as both characters find themselves on the wrong side of the bookcase in increasingly painful circumstances and instructing the other to put ... the candle ... *back*.

The Matrix Reloaded

In the Merovingian chateau, access to the dungeons is via a secret passage behind a bookcase that is opened by moving a copy of *Die Welt als Wille und Vorstellung* by Arthur Schopenhauer.

Real life

The library at Chatsworth House, the Derbyshire seat of the Duke of Devonshire, runs to some 40,000 books. At each end of the room, however, there are shelves containing books that don't exist. There are spines, immaculately bound and matching the rest of the library, but the titles in gilt are entirely fictional. *Racing Calendar Eclipse for 1831*, for instance, and *Shelley's Conchologist*. Some are pretty appalling gags: *Shadow Cabinets* by A. Ghost-Writer and *Reduced to the Ranks* by D. Motion being particularly egregious examples. The reason for these two shelves of non-sensical non-books is that they open to reveal spiral staircases that lead up to the next floor of the library. Additionally, in 2010 the current Duke was having a clear-out of the attics of the 300-room mansion when he came across a huge and ornate bookcase stored among the eaves. On closer inspection it was revealed to have a secret door installed. At some point, the bookcase had been built for and installed in Devonshire House before being moved to Chatsworth intended for the nursery. However, its providence dictated it was unsuitable for a child's room on the grounds that it had been built to provide illicit access between the bedrooms of the Prince Regent, who would become George IV, and his mistress Maria Fitzherbert.

'Digressions, incontestably, are the sunshine;- they are the life, the soul of reading;- take them out of this book, for instance,- you might as well take the book along with them.'

Laurence Sterne

Six weird book titles

Half Asleep in Frog Pajamas by Tom Robbins

Why Cats Paint: A Theory of Feline Aesthetics by Heather Busch and Burton Silver

How to Avoid Huge Ships by John W. Trimmer

Random Deaths and Custard by Catrin Dafydd

Bombproof Your Horse by Rick Pelicano

Living with Crazy Buttocks by Kaz Cooke

Bookshelves in style

In 2011 Karl Lagerfeld announced a new addition to his range of fragrances: 'Paper Passion', a perfume designed to smell like books. The smell of books, whether sharply brand new or mustily antiquarian, is a heady musk but if anyone could pull off such a literary fragrance it was Lagerfeld. At the time of his death in 2019, the designer boasted a personal library running to well over a quarter of a million books.

'Today I only collect books; there is no room left for anything else,' he said in 2015. 'If you go to my house there's a library of 300,000. It's a lot for an individual.'

Most of Lagerfeld's library was stored in a 20,000-square-foot, climate-controlled underground complex beneath the tennis court of his home in Biarritz.

'I am mad for books,' he said in 2010. 'It is a disease I won't recover from. They are the tragedy of my life.

I want to learn about everything and want to know everything but I'm not an intellectual and I don't like the company of intellectuals. I'm the most superficial man on earth.'

Perhaps the most notable thing about Lagerfeld's library – other than its sheer size – is that he stored the books on their sides in piles, which must have been a challenge if he wanted to read a book from near the bottom. Most of his library consisted of hardback books; according to friends, when Lagerfeld read a paperback, he tore each page out as he finished it.

Lagerfeld wasn't the only haute-couture bibliophile: Gianni Versace had five libraries, one in each of his homes, and employed a full-time librarian to look after them.

'There are perhaps no days of our childhood we lived so fully as those we believe we left without having lived them, those we spent with a favourite book.'

Marcel Proust

An early dog-ear

The phrase 'dog-eared', referring to a book that has had the corners of its pages turned down as markers, first appears in England in a 1737 poem by Thomas Tickell, a civil servant and a poet decent enough to be featured in Dr Johnson's *Lives of the Most Eminent English Poets* but generally forgotten now.

His poem 'The Horn-Book' – singing the praises of a kind of children's primer designed to help learn the alphabet and familiarise them with Bible stories in common use from the fifteenth century to the nineteenth – included this extract containing the first recorded reference to the dog-earing of pages:

But how shall I thy endless virtues tell
In which thou dost all other books excel?
No greasy thumbs thy spotless leaf can soil,
No crooked dog's ears thy smooth comers spoil;
In idle pages no errata stand
To tell the blunders of the printer's hand;
No fulsome dedication here is writ,
Nor flattering verse, to praise the author's
*   wit;*
The margin with no tedious notes is vext.
Nor various readings, to confound the text;
All parties in thy literal sense agree,
Thou perfect centre of concordancy!

The horse librarians
of Kentucky

In 1936 the United States Works Progress Administration introduced a scheme that was as ingenious as it was altruistic: the horse librarians of Kentucky. This hardy posse of literary riders was sent into the mountains, destined for some of the remotest communities in the country, carrying in their saddle-bags a selection of books to lend to and exchange with anyone who wanted them.

'That WPA was a big thing for us paupers,' one of the women, Grace Caudill Lucas, recalled in 1995. 'Everyone else thought of us as hillbillies, just poor, poor, poor.'

Lucas, a single mother at the time, was in her early twenties when she gave up work as a seamstress for the

161

outdoor life of a horse librarian, working three days a week for a pay packet of $28 a month. 'I had to pay 50 cents a day for my horse and I had to feed it too,' she grumbled.

Lucas would ride Bill, the black horse she was assigned, for mile after mile across treacherous terrain, picking her way along teetering mountain passes and fording rivers where the water lapped at her saddlebags, on a fortnightly round of individual homes and one-room schools where the children 'adored books like *Robinson Crusoe* and really loved poetry'.

The horse librarians were a feature of the rural Kentucky landscape until the WPA was disbanded in 1943 when US labour was refocused towards the war effort. During their seven years as itinerant librarians, the women distributed an estimated 3500 books and 8000 magazines every month. Even people who couldn't read liked to look at the pictures in the magazines and enjoyed having books read to them. Light fiction and cookery books – especially those concerned with canning and preserving food – were popular, and religious books were among the most borrowed. Nearly all the books were donated by organisations or individuals and they had an enormous impact on the communities they served.

'Learn me to read,' a seven-year-old boy bedbound with a serious spinal injury told a horse librarian in 1936, 'and then I won't be lonesome no more.'

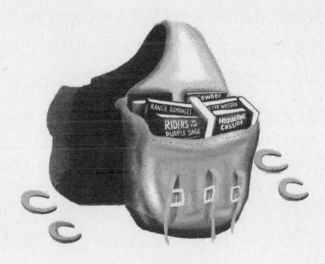

'Don't you ever mind,' she asked suddenly, 'not being rich enough to buy all the books you want?'

Edith Wharton

Five fictional bookshops

Flourish and Botts from the Harry Potter
novels by J.K. Rowling

The Shop Around The Corner from *You've Got
Mail*

Geiger's from *The Big Sleep* by Raymond
Chandler

Sempere & Sons from the *Cemetery of
Forgotten Books* series by Carlos Ruiz Zafón

Black Books from *Black Books*

Five great cinema bookshelves

The world of film is awash with notable bibliophiles. It's an old trope that, in order to make a character look thoughtful and intelligent (and occasionally completely insane), the easiest thing to do is stick a ginormous library in their home (or, in the case of the completely insane, their lair). Preferably this library would have beautifully crafted, floor-to-ceiling shelves packed with old, hardback, leather-bound books and a selection of leather-bound furniture in which the character can sit, read and look into the middle distance, stroking their chin while contemplating whatever challenging situation the script has directed their planet-sized brain towards. Usually, however, these people are evil geniuses.

Equally, the librarian is a notoriously one-dimensional figure in the hands of screenwriters. In the world of cinema it seems people who read books are nefarious, warped brainboxes awash with as much cash as their megalomania allows, while people who work with books are dullards frightened of their own shadows who have effectively ducked out of real life to hide among the stacks.

Despite this clear prejudice against book lovers, here are five great moments played out among cinematic bookshelves.

Breakfast at Tiffany's

There are few greater temples dedicated to the book than the New York Public Library in Manhattan, so it's no wonder the place has been a magnet for film-makers. From *Ghostbusters* to *The Day After Tomorrow*, the library has provided a bookish backdrop to a range of films – perhaps most notably the screen adaptation of Truman Capote's *Breakfast at Tiffany's*. It's the only place in which writer Paul Varjak feels entirely comfortable in the company of skittish socialite Holly Golightly, so it's fitting that he finally declares his love for her in one of its reading rooms. He spots Audrey Hepburn's Holly sitting at a table among a pile of hardback books, joins her, picks one up and bewilderedly announces its title to be *South America: Land of Wealth and Promise*, before a discussion arises during which he announces 'I love you' and is immediately shushed by another reader. It turns out, however, that Holly is in the library reading up on South America because she intends to marry a wealthy man called José da Silva Pereira.

The Mummy

Librarians generally get a raw deal from television and cinema. The men tend to be grumpy and nerdy, the women frumpy and nerdy. Think of Donna Reed's vivacious Mary in *It's A Wonderful Life* who – in the alternative story conjured by angel Clarence Odbody to show George Bailey what life would have been like without him – becomes a nervy, bespectacled spinster working in the town library. Rachel Weisz's Evelyn Carnahan in Stephen Sommer's 1999 film *The Mummy* might announce that she is proud of her profession – 'I . . . am a librarian!' – but she's still a stereotypically dotty, four-eyed boffin. Despite this, she is responsible for one of the great bookcase scenes in cinema. At the top of a ladder she finds a book misplaced on a high shelf and, trying to stretch across the void to the next case, she falls against it, setting off a spectacular round of bookcase dominoes as case falls against case all around the room, depositing the books all over the floor.

Interstellar

One of the most successful marryings of thrilling science-fiction cinema and actual proper science is Christopher Nolan's *Interstellar*. Matthew McConaughey is Coop, a man trying to help save a dying Earth by joining a mission into deep space lasting many years, much to the anguish of his daughter Murph. The plot is complicated but much of it revolves around a gravitational anomaly, the bending of time and the books on Murph's bedroom bookshelves that she believes are being tossed about by a poltergeist. This is probably the only film that turns a bookcase into a four-dimensional hypercubic tesseract ... or something.

Atonement

For all that we love books, few of us find bookshelves erotic. It's no coincidence that the phrase 'smouldering sexuality of the stacks' isn't in common usage despite being agreeably alliterative, and it's unlikely there's any kind of nookie going on in our nation's libraries as a kind of File High Club. Fortunately the magical world of cinema has no such qualms, and in the screen adaptation of Ian McEwan's *Atonement* Keira Knightley's Cecilia and James McAvoy's Robbie marble their endpapers against the shelves in the library of Cecilia's family home. Knightley later said, 'The best sex scene I've ever done on screen was that one, on the bookshelf.'

Star Wars: Attack of the Clones

In this 2002 instalment of the Star Wars franchise we see for the first time the Jedi Archives, the order's repository purported to contain the entire knowledge of the galaxy, sited on the planet Coruscant and run by the Council of First Knowledge. If its galleried stacks look familiar somehow it's because the Jedi Archive is based on the Long Room at the library of Trinity College in Dublin, right down to the busts of eminent people placed at the end of every stack. George Lucas was also possibly inspired to create the Archive by his own Lucasfilm Research Library, established a year after the first Star Wars film was released, in 1978. It soon outgrew his Los Angeles office so was moved to his house at Skywalker Ranch. It now includes almost 30,000 books and nearly 20,000 films as well as countless photographs, magazines and press cuttings. Although it's not open to the public, Lucasfilm staff can check out items just like at any regular library.

'We are of opinion that instead of letting books grow mouldy behind an iron grating, far from the vulgar gaze, it is better to let them wear out by being read.'

Jules Verne

A great fictional library

'The world ended for me the day my *Nautilus* dived for the first time beneath the waves,' said Captain Nemo to Professor Aronnax in Jules Verne's *Twenty Thousand Leagues Under the Sea*. 'On that day I bought my last volumes, my last pamphlets, my last newspapers, and since that time I would like to believe that mankind has neither thought nor written.' Verne's legendary submariner boasted a library of more than 12,000 books aboard his extraordinary, giant-squid-grappling vessel. The books were all bound in the same manner (how his bookbinder must have missed him once he'd vanished beneath the waves) and contained volumes on a range of topics in several languages, all stored on black rosewood bookcases with copper inlay. The library was furnished with a range of comfy leather chairs and sofas, not to mention a number of movable book stands to make the perusal of hefty volumes even more straightforward. He might have been nuts, but Captain Nemo certainly gives a person library goals.

'The reading of all good books is like conversation with the finest of the past centuries.'

René Descartes

The Brownings' bookcase

In the autumn of 1848 Elizabeth Barrett Browning wrote to a friend, 'When Robert and I are ambitious we talk about buying a whole edition of Balzac to put in our bookcase'. Later that year she wrote that they were 'expecting our books by an early vessel and are about to be very busy building up a rococo bookcase of carved angels and demons'. What made the Brownings' bookcase extra special was that it had been designed and built by Robert Browning himself. A keen joiner, Browning sourced three different oaks for his bookcase, ranging in age from the fifteenth to the seventeenth century. Eleven feet high, seven feet wide and eighteen inches deep, the bookcase included three drawers in which to house manuscripts of his own work.

'It is an immense advantage to bring the eye in aid of the mind; to see within a limited compass all the works that are accessible in a given library on a given subject; and to have the power of dealing with them collectively at a given spot, instead of hunting them up through an entire accumulation.'

William Ewart Gladstone

Ten fictional places in literature

Avonlea (*Anne of Green Gables* by Lucy Maud Montgomery)

Llareggub (*Under Milk Wood* by Dylan Thomas)

Raveloe (*Silas Marner* by George Eliot)

Macondo (*One Hundred Years of Solitude* by Gabriel García Márquez)

St Mary Mead (*Murder at the Vicarage* by Agatha Christie)

Barchester (*Barsetshire Chronicles* by Anthony Trollope)

Ten fictional places in literature

Weatherbury (*Far From the Madding Crowd* by Thomas Hardy)

Sleepy Hollow (*The Legend of Sleepy Hollow* by Washington Irving)

Maycomb (*To Kill a Mockingbird* by Harper Lee)

Bibliopolis (*The Great Pursuit* by Tom Sharpe)

'This is an important book, the critic assumes, because it deals with war. This is an insignificant book because it deals with the feelings of women in a drawing room.'

Virginia Woolf

All Greek to us

A contemporary of Christ, Seneca was a Roman statesman, philosopher and playwright who – despite having been dead for a shade under 2000 years – still has much to teach the bibliophile about the storage and display of their books.

'Let just as many books be acquired as are enough,' he said, 'but let none be just for show.'

Indeed, having books simply for the sake of owning them was something that grieved the Spanish-born Stoic greatly.

'How can you excuse the man who buys bookcases of expensive wood and piling into them the works of unknown, worthless authors goes yawning amongst his thousands of volumes?' he railed. 'He knows their titles, their bindings, but nothing else. It is in the homes of the idlest men that you find the biggest libraries – range upon range of books, piled as high as the ceiling. Nowadays a library is one of the essential fittings of a home, like a bathroom.'

Books, he insisted, were for reading, for expanding and improving the mind. They were not just there for show.

'You could forgive this if it were all due to a zeal for learning,' he wailed, clearly after a string of disappointing dinner parties where his efforts to engage the host in conversation about the contents of their libraries were met with blank looks. 'But these libraries of the works of piety and genius are collected for mere show, to ornament the walls of the house.'

'Each of us, when our day's work is done, must seek our ideal, whether it be love or pinochle or lobster à la Newburg, or the sweet silence of the musty bookshelves.'

O. Henry